P●WER
UP YOUR TRADIE BUSINESS
A BLUEPRINT FOR SUCCESS

MATTHEW JONES

For Mum and Dad, who have never
judged and always encouraged –
for which I will be forever grateful.

For my wife, Nicole, thank you for always
supporting and believing in me.

And for my sons, Ethan and Bryn,
who provide inspiration every day.

First published in 2017 by Matthew Jones

National Library of Australia Cataloguing-in-Publication entry:

Creator: Jones, Matthew, author.
Title: Power up your tradie business/Matthew Jones.
ISBN: 9781925648065 (paperback)
Subjects: Business planning.
New business enterprises – Management.
Entrepreneurship.
Success in business.

Project management and text design by Michael Hanrahan Publishing
Cover design by Peter Reardon

Disclaimer

Contents

STAGE 1: CLARITY

STAGE 2: CONTROL

STAGE 4: CONNECTION

Introduction

ENSLAVED TO THE JOB

I looked at myself in the mirror with tears welling in my eyes. I felt like a failure, overwhelmed and angry. I had no money in the bank, bills were piled high and I had mouths to feed. On top of that, I had just received a letter from a liquidator stating that the debt collector I had engaged to recover $30,000 owing from my builder client had gone into liquidation. You have got to be kidding me, right? The debt collection company has gone bankrupt? No! The debt collector had also taken me for the $3000 I paid them to recover my $30,000. So I was $33,000 down. I was done.

This position of despair that I found myself in early 1997 was a culmination of all the choices I had made during the preceding seven years operating my plumbing business. My problem was not that the customer didn't pay or that the debt collector went broke. The problem was me. Looking into the mirror I could see history repeating again. Win some, lose some. Boom, bust. Money in the bank, no money in the bank. In control, out of control. Great clients, Mr. Creature clients (more on them later). I can do this, I can't do this. Who am I kidding?

It hit me at that moment I needed to make drastic changes fast. I couldn't keep running in survival mode year on year. The excitement of starting the business – with its promise of providing personal and financial freedom – was a distant memory. In its place was frustration and anger. I started the business because I wanted to run my own show, to have control of my own destiny. However, right now I was out of control.

This brought a lot of questions to the surface. How did I get myself into a situation where I had created a job for myself that enslaved me? How come clients did not value the work we delivered? Why did clients keep coming back trying to drive down the price? Why did it seem the harder I worked, the less money I was making? Why was it that being great on the tools and delivering great work didn't automatically convert to money in the bank?

BETTER AT BUSINESS

At this point I realised being great on the tools was not enough – I had to be great at business. And to become great at business, I needed serious change. I had to put my hand up and admit I needed help – something that was not commonplace in the construction game at the time. What would my old South African boss who I started my plumbing apprenticeship with in the 1980s have thought if I showed any sign of weakness? Back then, it was work hard, and then work harder. It was get on the shovel and dig. It wasn't asking questions; it was just saying yes and getting on with it. It was being grateful for what you have, or getting kicked up the bum. No whinging, just do it.

Putting my hand up for help, even though I was at my lowest point, gave me a huge sense of relief, because I knew I could change my destiny. I could get control and make positive change. Rather than looking at my past as a series of failures, I changed my view to seeing it as the harsh learning experience I needed at that very moment in time. I knew this experience was going to make me a stronger person, and was an investment in the university of life.

I began feeling the same excitement that I experienced when I originally started my plumbing business, which had been extinguished a long time ago.

'This is it,' I told myself, and I made a promise to myself that never again would I be in this situation of helplessness. Never again would I rely on other people for my own success. Never again would I lack belief in myself. Never again would I surround myself with people who wanted to keep me down.

Now was the time to put my future plans into action. I began to feel sick as my head raced with all kinds of crazy ideas and self-doubts. I had to push them aside, however, and remind myself I was hungry to be great at business. I was hungry to learn what it takes to be great at business. I was hungry to provide a great life-style for my family.

Three months after receiving the letter notifying me the debt collector I had engaged was going into liquidation, I closed my plumbing business. I began applying for corporate jobs and tertiary study even though I couldn't turn on a computer, and I didn't even know what the internet was. This was scary, because change is scary. The last time I studied was when I completed my advanced plumbing at TAFE. At the time, I remember thinking, *You beauty! This is the last time I ever have to study.* Looking back now, I am thankful that I was very wrong.

LEARN EVERY DAY

After I closed my plumbing business, something happened that changed my life forever. I enrolled in a community college evening course to learn how to use a computer. The course ran for one night a week for 13 weeks. It was literally basic stuff like here is the power cord, plug it into the socket, turn on the computer, this is the keyboard. However, this was the best $395 investment I had ever made. From that moment, as I started to learn about things that had previously scared me, I began to love learning. I began to understand that once you opened yourself up to the learning process, it became easy and very enjoyable. I became hungry to learn, and I wanted more.

Over the next 10 years I immersed myself in learning as much as I could about business and personal success. I had the opportunity to be exposed to the boardrooms of several multinational organisations in general management roles, accountable for delivering $100 million in revenue and inspiring teams of 200. At the same time, I challenged myself to complete my formal studies, earning a Bachelor of Business and Commence Degree from university, and an advanced business diploma. On a daily basis I also loved listening to or reading performance and success thought leaders such as Jim Rohn, Stephen Covey, Michael Gerber, Jack Welch, and Richard Branson. It totally opened my eyes. Awesome.

ABOUT THIS BOOK

This book shares all my business experiences and learnings gained over some 25 years. Throughout my journey I discovered a 'Blueprint for Success' that I developed into a four-stage framework. Since 2007, the Blueprint for Success program has been delivered to successfully help over 5000 tradie business owners build a business that successfully generates profit and provides for a great lifestyle. The step-by-step framework educates and guides business owners how to successfully make the transition off the tools and onto the business by working smarter not harder. The four stages of the Blueprint for Success framework are Clarity, Control, Confidence and Connection, and these stages also form the framework for this book. The first part of the book looks at the five most common mistakes tradies make, including giving into what I've termed the 'tradie mindset syndrome', working harder not smarter and avoiding change.

The next four parts of the book are aligned with the four stages of the Blueprint for Success framework. Here's a rundown of what each part focuses on, and how each stage leads to the next:

- *Clarity:* The important question a business owner must ask is, 'What must the business deliver my family to ensure the investment provides adequate returns?' In other words, what is the longer term vision or objective of the business? With clear vision comes clarity relating to what the business must stand for in terms of culture, behaviour, values and beliefs. I sum all this up with 'the way we do it here' – the non-negotiable operating DNA of the business. With this clarity comes focused effort, which in turn guarantees profit goals are achieved through the business investing in the right systems and attracting the right type of customer and team members.

- *Control:* Clarity helps you identify the key areas of the business that must be recorded and reported on, on a regular basis. If a process cannot be reported on, it cannot be measured. Without measurement, you can't control the business. This part helps you identify the required reporting tools and measurement to give you the necessary control across finances, marketing, team and processes. Put simply, like any sporting team, you need to check the scoreboard and review your stats to understand what areas are working or not working. This knowledge drives continual performance improvement, a prerequisite for survival in the competitive and brutal landscape all businesses operate in today.

- *Confidence:* With control comes the confidence to make educated decisions quickly. You don't experience procrastination, second guessing or, importantly, lack of belief. Confidence gives you the power to make great decisions. Your decision-making framework relates to how to price for profit, when to hire and fire, when to say no to dodgy customers, and when to reinvest into the business. Your confidence then flows through the entire business into team members, customers, suppliers and partners. All stakeholders have the confidence and the belief that the business will deliver a consistent customer experience and a consistent financial return.

- *Connection:* Businesses that radiate confidence attract great opportunities and great partnerships. Once you have mastered clarity, control and confidence, you can position your business to leverage social and community networks, industry events and partnerships. With connection comes the opportunity to become a key person of influence in your chosen market – the expert, the go-to person. This attraction is possible because the business is making a positive contribution back into the community.

Adding to my business experiences and learnings, my company also conducted extensive research of 466 trade service and construction business owners, using our 'Score Your Business' assessment. Businesses researched included plumbing, gas fitting, electrical, building, air-conditioning, refrigeration, tiling, landscaping, plastering, and motor mechanics. This research enriched my understanding of what factors contribute to a blueprint for success. Ultimately, I wanted to identify and confirm the key processes and systems that, if implemented correctly, would guarantee the business owner achieved their personal goals. The findings from this research, which supported my belief relating to what constitutes business success, formed the basis for writing this book. The findings from this research in specific areas are shared throughout the book.

In my business, I've chosen to partner with organisations that, like me, want their customers to be successful in business and in life. The partners I choose need to see themselves as being able to add value to their customers' businesses, rather than seeing themselves as simply suppliers of boxes filled with widgets.

Reece (plumbing and building suppliers), Telstra (through their Trades Assist work management software system), and Burson Auto Parts (auto mechanical suppliers) are some of the premium brands I work with that are willing to invest in their customers' business education to enable improved performance, assisting customers throughout their business journey to become more productive and profitable.

These organisations understand the necessity of transitioning from a traditional 'customer–supplier transaction' to a 'business partnership relationship', moving away from being a simple supplier of boxes filled with widgets, to becoming a vested partner creating win–win partnerships for all.

Through partnering with these organisations, I have had the opportunity to communicate our Blueprint for Success message and framework to tens of thousands of business owners. I also share case studies from these partnerships through this book.

MY VISION TO GUARANTEE SUCCESS

My vision is that every business should have the opportunity to be successful. The problem for tradie business owners is often that they 'don't know what they don't know' in relation to understanding what it takes to build a successful business. My aim is to create a lightbulb moment for all tradie business owners so they can, firstly, see what is required to be successful at business and, secondly, understand how they can be successful at business.

My philosophy is simple: with the right thinking and the right business intelligence I believe no business should fail. In other words, with the right thinking, the right business information can be interpreted to make great decisions to guarantee a profitable, sustainable business.

I am passionate about making positive change and playing a part in assisting business owners to improve the overall professionalism within the construction and trade service industry. The more professional a business's operations are, the greater the chance of financial success, the greater the opportunity to contribute to the community and, ultimately, the greater the quality of life for all.

This book is designed to build your knowledge and understanding as you work through each stage of the Blueprint for Success framework. Each stage builds on the previous stage to assist you in developing the Clarity, Control, Confidence and Connection you need to build a great business and give yourself a great life.

As a business owner, your duty is to be successful, so don't settle for mediocrity. Get excited about being more successful than you could ever imagine.

PART I

The five great mistakes made by tradies

Over the course of my 25-year business journey, I have identified five common mistakes made by many tradie business owners. These mistakes limit the performance of the business, reducing profit and cash flow and often leading to business failure. Operating a successful tradie business in the information and technology age we now live in requires a new level of thinking and awareness.

Our goal as business owners is to build a profitable and sustainable business that satisfies our personal goals for decades. To achieve this, you must not submit to the traditional way of thinking – where you only need to work hard on the tools and, by default, the business will be successful. You must be aware of your operating mindset to ensure you do not create a job for yourself where everything revolves around you. This leads to being busy all the time, increased stress and a lack of motivation.

When you are operating in this state, you are constantly putting out fires to survive the day, with no thought given to the long term. Your focus is all about working hard to get a lot of tasks done, rather than working intelligently to get the right tasks done. Work often comes down to quantity over quality due to a lack of focus and priorities. Everything appears urgent and important. Any potential change within the business is avoided because operating the business has become hard enough without adding to the work load.

Do not mistake activity for productivity. You may be spinning faster and faster on the hamster wheel, but you are not moving towards achieving your personal goals.

CHAPTER 1

Submitting to the 'Tradie Mindset Syndrome'

DON'T BECOME ENSLAVED TO THE JOB

I still remember the excitement of receiving the business cards for my first business. I was very proud to be going it alone. I was sick of working hard making money for other people, and I was over having to answer to other people. I thought that because I was good on the tools and I knew how to solve a lot of plumbing problems, I would instantly be financially rewarded. This was my chance to earn a lot of money and have personal freedom. Or so I thought.

I was highly motivated when I started my business. I said yes to everyone who knocked on my door. I tested my hand at new types of work and new types of clients. A lot of the time I was learning on the run, and I made a lot of mistakes that cost me a lot of money – for example, underestimating the required labour hours, underestimating the required materials, incorrectly installing systems or incorrectly hiring people. These mistakes resulted in me having to work harder to make up for the loss of money and loss of time. Because I was losing money my bank balance was constantly in the red, meaning I had no cash flow. Unbeknown to me at the time, I was infected with what I have termed the 'tradie mindset syndrome'.

Cap in hand is fatal

Having no money in the bank meant I was under constant pressure to do more work. The bills were piling up fast. I owed my suppliers, had payments due for my car lease, phone, wages, and the list goes on. I didn't care what I was charging for the job, I just had to win the job. I was often going 'cap in hand' to builders and property managers, asking for any work they could give me. This was a huge mistake, and one that is common to many tradies.

When you go 'cap in hand', you are basically on your knees begging for work. For a business owner, this is a fatal position. You are stressed, often unable to sleep. Your decision-making is poor, due to all the decisions you make being reactive to the current situation. Every decision is based on surviving today, and you can give little to no thought to the potentially negative impact this decision will have on the business next week, next month or next year.

This is one of the first symptoms of the 'tradie mindset syndrome': the business owner is operating in survival mode, week to week, month to month, year to year. If you're in this mode, you're operating like a fire chief putting out fires, where everything is important and everything is urgent. Nothing ever gets done to a great standard, the client experience changes day to day, clients never receive great service, and team members come and go. Action is incorrectly mistaken for productivity and profit.

When you're operating like this, your business quickly becomes irrelevant in today's market. You never become known as the expert in solving a particular problem, and your business never 'wows' clients. Your business doesn't create brand advocates – those customers who proactively promote the business – and doesn't inspire team members. Your business never attracts great talent or business partners, and always competes on price.

Inadvertently, when you're operating from within the tradie mindset syndrome, you've become enslaved to the job. You can't step away from the business because everything revolves around you. Rather than creating a business that serves you in delivering profit and lifestyle, you've created a job that's suffocating you.

Everything revolves around you as the business owner. Every day I speak with owners who state they are burnt out, tired and frustrated because they can't step away from the business. If they step away, the business stops. At this stage, they ultimately realise they don't have a business at all. They just have a job.

All this is a result of the tradie mindset syndrome, characterised by the following thinking:

- I only need to be good on the tools and the business will be successful.

- I only have to work hard to get ahead financially.

- The busier I am, the more profit I will be making.

- I do not have time to plan my future; my priority is to get the job done.

- I do not have time to review my financial performance; my priority is to get the job done.

- I must say yes to every customer.

- I must calculate my price to ensure I win the work.

- I am focused on turnover and do not consider profit.

- My business is different from all others.

- I can do it alone.

This way of thinking quickly turns the excitement of creating a new business – created to provide personal and financial freedom – into a nightmare of frustrations. As the owner, you're quickly trapped like a hamster on the wheel – spinning faster and faster, but not going anywhere. Starting work in the early hours of the morning and finishing the paperwork late every night after the kids are in bed. Quality family time happens less and less, and family holidays are not a priority (or not even possible). Even when physically at home, you're not present in mind, because you're constantly thinking about the job.

The real horror of the situation presents itself when, after all that hard work, your accountant calculates what you owe to the tax-man – and you have absolutely no money in the bank to pay the tax bill. This is not fun. This is not a business. This has no future. And the realisation sets in that you've created a job you are enslaved to. I liken this situation to driving a car at night in the pitch black with no lights, unaware you are driving next to a cliff.

Knowing what your time is worth

When calculating the huge number of hours you invest in spinning the wheel of your business, you need to take into account all activities – including time invested in quoting on and setting up the job, getting the team organised, travelling, completing the job, invoicing the job, paying the wages, paying suppliers, hiring and firing, and following up outstanding payments. When measuring the total hours invested against the actual money earned, I have calculated some business owners' financial returns can be as low as $10 per hour.

When viewing your financial return, you also need to consider the level of financial investment required, and the associated risk in undertaking the chosen work. Here lies the real problem: your required financial return as the business owner, based on the level of investment, is rarely, if ever, considered. Why? Because from the start your only consideration was getting away from working a job created by someone else, and working a job created by you. I repeat, work a job created by you. This is all about the job, which focuses on turnover, not about the business – which focuses on financial return on investment.

It is at this stage, however, the business is on life support. You're tired and not sure how long you can keep going. Every day feels like groundhog day, over and over. You often have little to show for all the blood, sweat and tears you've invested. The bank balance is not where it should be. The level of your personal savings and investment is not where it should be. The number of family holiday and adventure memories is not where it should be.

Understanding the risks when operating a business

When the business is on life support, the next step for most tradie business owners is to shut the doors. Depending on where you source statistics from, between 60 and 80 per cent of trade and construction businesses fail or shut down within the first five years of starting out. This is an incredibly daunting figure – especially when you consider that during that first five-year period the business owner commonly went through periods of not drawing a regular wage. During this period, the business owner invested vast amounts of time and money. By the time the business owner shuts the doors after running out of energy and cash, they are highly likely to have not broken even on their investment.

You need to think of your business as any investment – whether the investment be property, shares or your business, you require a financial return on top of the initial investment based on the level of risk exposure. And when it comes to operating a business, the risk exposure is high.

Score Your Business:
How satisfied are business owners?

As mentioned in the Introduction, I asked 466 trades and construction business owners to complete my 'Score Your Business' assessment to gain a greater understanding of the level of satisfaction among business owners in relation to financial return and lifestyle.

The high-level findings relating to business owner satisfaction based on level of turnover and years of operation are shown in the following tables and analysis.

Level of turnover

The breakdown of businesses that participated in the assessment based on annual turnover is shown in the following table.

Turnover	Total	As % of total
Less than $300K	245	53%
$300K–$600K	112	24%
$600K–$1M	59	13%
More than $1M	50	11%
Total	466	100%

The key point to note from the preceding table is that 53 per cent of participating businesses had less than $300,000 turnover annually.

The assessment then looked at business owner's levels of satisfaction, with the question, 'Are you satisfied that you are achieving your personal goals? (Such as lifestyle, income, debt levels, working hours and stress level.)' The following table shows satisfaction levels based on turnover breakdowns.

Turnover	Satisfied	As % of category total
Less than $300K	72	29%
$300K–$600K	27	24%
$600K–$1M	11	19%
More than $1M	12	24%
Total	**122**	**26%**

The key points here are:

- Overall, only 26 per cent of business owners are satisfied that they are achieving their personal goals relating to lifestyle choices, financial position, and pressure levels. This means a huge 74 per cent of business owners are not satisfied in what their business is currently delivering to their personal lives. Increasing turnover doesn't increase the level of satisfaction.

- Only 24 per cent of business owners turning over greater than $1,000,000 are satisfied that they are achieving their personal goals. This is fewer than the 26 per cent overall who are satisfied. This highlights that, as the business grows, the owner is drowning in the day-to-day tasks due to a lack of understanding relating to the administrative processes and systems required to deliver the increased workload.

Years of operation

The breakdown of businesses that participated in the assessment based on years of operation is shown in the following table.

Years operating	Total	As % of total
Fewer than 1	105	23%
1	24	5%
1–3	103	22%
3–5	57	12%
More than 5	176	38%
Total	**466**	**100%**

The key point here is that 38 per cent of respondents have been operating for greater than five years.

The following table breaks down responses to the question on owner satisfaction ('Are you satisfied that you are achieving your personal goals? Such as lifestyle, income, debt levels, working hours and stress level.') based on years operating.

Years operating	Satisfied	As % of category total
Fewer than 1	43	41%
1	7	29%
1 to 3	25	24%
3 to 5	13	23%
More than 5	34	19%
Total	122	26%

The key point to note from the findings here is that as the length of time the owner has been operating their business increases, year on year, the level of satisfaction declines. For those business owners who have been operating for greater than five years, satisfaction levels dropped to only 19 per cent being satisfied. The longer the business operates, the more tired the owner becomes.

SATISFACTION STARTS WITH THINKING

Why are the business shutdown rates so high? Why are 74 per cent of business owners not satisfied? Why are 81 per cent of those business owners operating for more than five years not satisfied? To a large part, these results are because of mindset. The owner is operating in the wrong mindset. Mindset dictates your thinking. Your thinking directs your actions. Your actions drive your results.

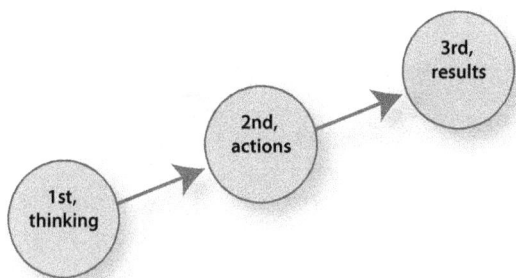

When I state this to my clients, their first reaction is usually push back. 'My business isn't underperforming because of my mindset,' they might say. 'My business is underperforming due to the economy being down' – or government regulation adding costs to operate the business, stiff competition, clients being all about price, suppliers being too expensive, not being able to find the right team members, accountants providing poor advice, the newspapers stating doom and gloom. The list goes on and on.

What we have here is the 'tradie mindset syndrome' talking. *I am the victim in all this, it is not my fault.* Get over it and make a choice to instead adopt a 'business performance mindset'. Business owners who operate in the business performance mindset build great businesses, no matter what they are facing in their operating environment.

Businesses that consistently perform at high levels are the direct result of the business owner operating in a business performance mindset. Great businesses consistently deliver a great financial return, offer a great lifestyle of choice, and are great contributors to the community. This is achieved despite what is going on around them.

View of the world

Why is mindset so critical? Because it determines how you view the world. Look at the following table to test how you currently view the world. What lens do you view the world through?

Situation	Tradie mindset syndrome view	Business performance mindset view
Approach to business	Job that is a means to an end	Business is an investment that must deliver a financial return
Submitting a quote with no future jobs in the pipeline	Price to win the work; will cut corners when needed	Price for profit with no short cuts – do not compromise
Business is underperforming	Have an external focus and believe performance is out of my control	Have an internal focus and understand performance is controllable
Desired success not yet achieved	The goal is the destination and when I get there only then will I be happy	Understand business is a journey and success is defined by who you become
Hiring and retaining great team members is hard	Ignore the issue and simply put it down to not being able to find anyone like me	Learn to understand why this is happening – develop brand and people solutions
Meeting a customer to follow up a quote	See it as an obligation and not having the time to waste	See it as an opportunity to build a relationship – ensure the best solution is provided

Situation	Tradie mindset syndrome view	Business performance mindset view
Arriving to a new job	Think about transaction only and completing the job as quickly as possible to go to next job	Think partnership and understanding customer's needs to convert to a lifetime client
Investing in the business	Fear of failure due to short-term thinking; cannot see value in the investment	100% belief that it is the right decision for the business's long-term success
Requiring assistance to grow the business	Want to go it alone, thinking that no-one else can understand the business	Understand importance of having a support team of external parties to safely guide the business

Even if you're predominately viewing the world through the lens of the tradie mindset syndrome, your mindset can always change. Once you understand that your decision-making and your performance are a result of your subconscious thinking, you can begin to consciously think differently.

The aim of this book is to turn the lights on for business owners, getting you out of the dark of the past and into the light of future opportunity. Once you understand the business performance mindset, you are on the path to building a great business. Based on my life and business experiences, I believe this to be true 100 per cent.

History lesson: Global financial crisis

Before the global financial crisis (GFC) in 2008, everything was great. Most business owners had no need to worry, with lots of work rolling in and easy money. Business was easy. So a lot of business owners became complacent, taking their eyes off the wheel while the business was steering its own course. They didn't need to check the performance of the business because money was easy to come by. Besides, if they became short of cash the banks were giving it away.

Then the GFC hit with a bang. *Shit, I didn't see that coming*, was what most business owners thought. The economy was busted. Business models were busted. Thinking was busted. Carnage everywhere, with huge financial, social and moral costs. Why did this happen? For most tradie business owners, it was because they were operating with their heads in the 'tradie mindset syndrome' cloud, thinking that the good times would roll on forever.

Learn from history: booms and busts will always occur. Those business owners operating with a business performance mindset are preparing for the next bust. They take nothing for granted. They are preparing their business to weather the storm that will hit some time in the future. They are preparing their business to be resilient. They are preparing their business to be sustainable well into the future.

PATH OF LEAST RESISTANCE

Humans will always take the path of least resistance. It's in our make-up. If we're faced with a choice, we'll most likely take the easier option. For a tradie, the easy option is to focus on the job. When faced with the choice between spending time reviewing the financial numbers of the business and doing the job, doing the job always wins. When faced with the choice to either spend time creating a plan that will guarantee long-term success or doing the job, doing the job always wins.

Why? Because doing the job comes easy; it is what a tradie is good at, it is natural. It is the path of least resistance. Working on the business is new, and does not come naturally. Doing the business thing is hard. Choosing the path of least resistance, however, is 'tradie mindset syndrome' thinking.

As a business owner, you must be operating in the business performance mindset to challenge the path of least resistance. The business performance mindset ensures owners make the tough calls – tough calls that will create short-term pain, but deliver long-term profitable gain. This way of thinking understands that taking the easy options in life leads to fool's gold.

In *The Ultimate Blueprint for an Insanely Successful Business*, Keith Cunningham frames the basic difference between the tradie mindset syndrome and the business performance mindset. Cunningham states great operators get tired while great business owners get rich. Your choice: do you want to be a great operator or a great business owner?

Your takeaways

1. Look out for tradie mindset syndrome thinking – instead, operate with business performance mindset thinking.

2. Focus on your desired financial return of investment, rather than focusing on being busy.

3. Understand your mindset determines your view of the world and your actions – and that you can consciously change your mindset.

4. Avoid the path of least resistance, and instead choose short-term pain for long-term gain.

CHAPTER 2

Working hard rather than intelligently

MY STORY

When running a trade service business, it is very easy to work hard. Yes, I am saying working hard is easy. We are taught from the moment we commence an apprenticeship that the job is all about hard work. Keep your head down, work hard, ask no questions. This becomes ingrained into the way we operate, part of our DNA; our focus is on getting a lot done in a day. As we progress to a tradesman and then venture into our own business, we are hardwired into thinking that if we are busy all day, we must be productive. Wrong.

Why do I believe this is wrong? Because this kind of thinking leads to too many tradie businesses failing. In my plumbing business, I was mentally stuck in the tradie mindset syndrome of working hard at all costs. Thinking that I had to have a lot of work – any work – on all the time. Thinking that I needed to keep the boys busy, no matter what. Thinking that being busy and working hard all the time is the only way to financially get ahead. Thinking that I couldn't afford to spend time in the office to understand where we are making money or losing money. Crazy.

Here I was thinking that I could not stop for even one day to analyse the performance of the business. I felt guilty if I wasn't onsite with our team, in the grind, getting the job done. Dig up, lay the sewer, lay the stormwater, back fill. Strip the roof, lay the new roof. Strip a house, rough in, fit off. At all times, I felt I needed to be shoulder to shoulder with the boys because I wanted to lead from the front. When faced with a choice, I took the path of least resistance and jumped into the job.

The problem for me was that I became so invested in the job that I had no idea which type of work generated the most profit. I didn't know which clients generated the most profit. I worked for commercial property managers, residential builders, real estate agents, government and the local Mr and Mrs Jones. Because my goal was to be busy, getting things done, I viewed every job and every client the same. I couldn't prioritise my time effectively, I didn't know which customers to say no to, I had no idea what the business really stood for, and I had no idea which direction to take the business.

I found working hard to get a lot of things done the easy part of running the business. Operating in the 'fire chief' mode, where everything is urgent and important, was easy for me. Reacting to every phone call that came through was easy. The hard part was saying no. The hard part was slowing down to review, measure and analyse the performance of the business.

With this type of information, what I now call your business scorecard, I could have made educated business decisions. Yes, I knew that if I had this information I could work more intelligently by the simple fact I would be making better quality decisions. Again, your aim is to do the most amount of intelligent work, not simply the most amount of work.

However, I found working intelligently very hard for several reasons. To start with, I didn't know how to record, collate or report the required information. I didn't have the financial intelligence to then understand and interpret the information. Finally, I thought focusing on this area was a waste of time because if I wasn't onsite I couldn't charge myself out and therefore it was costing me money.

Becoming a more effective leader

Stephen Covey, in his bestseller *The 7 Habits of Highly Effective People*, explains working intelligently as 'sharpening the saw'. Covey shares the story of the woodcutter who, on his first day, cuts down 18 trees. His boss, who pays well and provides good working conditions, encourages the woodcutter to keep up the good work, and the woodcutter is motivated to do so. His tally each day, however, begins to decrease, even though he is working harder. The woodcutter goes to his boss to apologise. His boss responds as follows:

'When was the last time you sharpened your axe?' the boss asked.

'Sharpen? I had no time to sharpen my axe. I have been very busy trying to cut trees ...'

Covey states that our lives are like this. We sometimes get so busy that we don't take time to sharpen the 'saw' (or in the case of the woodcutter in the preceding story, sharpen the axe). In today's world, it seems that everyone is busier than ever, but less happy than ever. Why is that? Could it be that we have forgotten how to stay 'sharp'? Nothing is wrong with activity and hard work. However, we all need time to relax, to think and meditate, and to learn and grow. If we don't take the time to sharpen the 'saw', we will become dull and lose our effectiveness.

In the context of operating a business, sharpening the saw relates to your effectiveness as a leader, the quality of your systems, and the motivation levels of your team. As a leader, you must continually sharpen your decision-making process through investing the time to ensure all financial, job and customer data is accurate and up to date. With quality information and data, you must then collate and report your results into a scoreboard. Your scoreboard allows you to analyse your performance, highlighting which areas of your business require 'sharpening'.

THE CONCEPT OF A SCORECARD

The facts showing how your business is operating become your scorecard. With a scorecard, you can quickly see where you are making money and losing money. Your scorecard highlights the areas where the 'saw' needs to be sharpened, where investment is required to upgrade the saw, and the areas where the saw needs to be scrapped all together. Simply, the scorecard shows you what is working and what not is working.

I know what you are thinking: *That's great but how do I create my scoreboard?* In my business, I developed 'The CUBE', which is a business intelligence software platform that empowers business owners and operators by delivering real-time business intelligence by way of looking at all sides of the business at once. The CUBE aims to provide business owners with instant, complete business information by analysing current job data, accounts data, individual data and customer data all at once. This current data is measured against performance targets, which then calculates the business's predicted results. The CUBE is also designed to enable real-time proactive decision-making through identifying the priority tasks and directing what action needs to be taken. The CUBE provides business owners with Clarity amid the chaos of running the day-to-day operations (covered in part II of this book), with Control through detailed measurement and analysis to ensure the business is performing as planned (part III), and with the Confidence to make the right decisions required to position the business for long-term success (part IV).

I discuss the ideas that were behind the development of The CUBE software throughout this book, and how you can focus on the same areas to create your scorecard and so improve your data analysis and decision-making. At this point, it is important to understand that an accurate and up-to-date scorecard is the key to working intelligently. Through parts II to V of this book, we will work through the steps required to build your scoreboard to commence working intelligently 'on the business', and less 'on the tools'.

STAND BACK AND OBSERVE

As a business leader, if you do not sharpen the saw, your individual performance and decision-making will become dull and ineffective. This will translate into your team's performance being dull and ineffective, resulting in a poorly performing business. Think about this: why do professional sporting teams review every play, review every decision and review every player after every game? Because the coach knows he (or she) needs to know the areas to improve if they are to compete next game, or if they are to compete for the championship. The coach understands their role is not to be on the field with the players to help kick, pass or tackle. The coach's role is to observe, reflect, review and compare performance so they can discuss and collaborate with the team where, why and how they need to sharpen the saw.

Early in Sir Alex Ferguson's coaching career, before he become the most successful football coach in history while guiding Manchester United, he spent most of his time being hands-on, training the players on the field. In Ferguson's book *Leading*, he explains his transition from the pitch to the stands, acknowledging that a more distant observer can sometimes see the bigger picture better than a coach on the field. Ferguson talks about his initial reluctance to delegate on-field training to his assistant manager, but came to realise it was the 'best thing' he ever did:

It didn't take away my control. My presence and ability to super-vise were always there, and what you can pick up by watching is incredibly valuable. Once I stepped out of the bubble, I became more aware of a range of details, and my performance level jumped. Seeing a change in a player's habits or a sudden dip in his enthu-siasm allowed me to go further with him: Is it family problems? Is he struggling financially? Is he tired? What kind of mood is he in? Sometimes I could even tell that a player was injured when he thought he was fine.

I don't think many people fully understand the value of observing. I came to see observation as a critical part of my management skills. The ability to see things is key or, more specifically, the ability to see things you don't expect to see.

OLYMPIC LESSONS

When I was growing up in Maroubra I aspired to be an Olympian. My goal was to represent Australia in sprint kayak paddling. I knew I had to work hard. I knew I had to get up early. I knew I had to paddle over 150 kilometres per week. I knew I had to lift tonnes of weights per gym session. I knew I had to cross-train with running, riding and swimming. I knew I had to keep my body in shape with stretching and yoga. Through working hard my times improved, I got on the medal dais at the Australian Championships, and I rep-resented Australia. However, working hard alone was not enough to achieve my dream of becoming an Olympian.

I got caught up in doing the 'what' – in other words, simply ticking boxes. Ticking off sessions per week, ticking off kilometres churned out on the water, ticking off tonnes lifted in the gym. I thought that if I just kept ticking the 'what' boxes, I would continue to improve. Simple – just keep doing more of the same. Over time when I noticed my times were getting slower my fallback position was to work harder. Get up earlier, do more sessions, and increase the length of these sessions. More of the 'what'. Unfortunately, this didn't help my performance. I ended up becoming fatigued and sick due to the lack of rest and recovery.

My quest

Not until after failing to realise my Olympic dream and finally hanging up my paddle did I start to reflect on my performances. I started asking questions. Why did I miss out and why did others with the same ability as me make selection? I entered into a quest to understand what it takes to consistently perform at a great level. What it takes to climb the Everest of winning an Olympic gold medal, and then return to the summit four years later.

I spent two years picking the brain of a former Hungarian Olympic coach. Hungarians, along with Germans, are the dominate powerhouses of sprint kayak paddling, consistently delivering gold medals at every Olympics. I studied Tudor Bompa, regarded as the 'godfather of periodisation training' – which focuses on planning training cycles that will guarantee peak performance at the right times. I began testing and measuring my learnings with the squad of athletes I was coaching. One of the athletes I coached was Tate Smith, who went on to win an Olympic gold medal at the 2012 London Olympic Games.

Rather than direct these athletes on 'what' to do, I wanted to empower them through helping them understand 'why' they were doing it. This was a huge shift – away from the traditional coaching model of just 'do what I say', toward intelligent coaching through empowering the athlete to think about 'why' they were doing what they were doing.

During this period, I noted that for most athletes, again, working hard is very easy. It is part of their DNA. It is who they are. Working hard is what has allowed them to achieve a level of success – be it in local, national or international competition. Working hard is what comes naturally. For the most part, the athlete doesn't have to think too hard, just do 'what' the coach says.

However, to achieve a greater level of success, or to maintain a level of success, you must ask 'why'. Why am I doing this session? Why is this session important to achieving my long-term goal? Why is rest important?

At this point I realised athletes find stopping and questioning 'why' hard. It is far simpler to continue working hard on the 'what'. This is their path of least resistance. I framed this as 'training hard is easy; training intelligently is hard.' Most athletes are unaware that they are stuck in this way of thinking. Most athletes mistake activity for productivity. To me, productivity is making forward progress toward achieving the goal. Just doing a lot of training sessions doesn't guarantee the athlete will move toward their goals.

Intelligent operator

Lachlan Tame is to me an example of what training intelligently looks like. Lachlan Tame represented Australia at the 2016 Rio Olympic Games, winning a bronze medal in the K2 1000-metre event (K2 refers to a two-man kayak). Lachlan partnered with Ken Wallace in the event. In the final at the Olympic Games, eight nations were lined up in their respective lanes, looking straight down the 1000-metre course. Each of the finalists had a different story for how they ended up on the start line, but each had invested the last four years to perform at their peak at this very moment in time. They had invested lots of hard work, and endured lots of ups and downs. Now it was down to this one race.

I began coaching Lachlan in 2008 when he was an ocean surf ski paddler competing at Surf Life Saving competitions. In 2010 Lachlan began to dip his toe into the water of flatwater kayak paddling. (Ocean surf ski paddlers commonly cross-over to flatwater kayak paddling, and vice versa.) Flatwater kayak paddling requires greater endurance and solid technique because competitors receive no assistance from the ocean. By 2011, after winning the Australian surf ski championship, Lachlan made a commitment to represent Australia at the Olympics in 2016. His Olympic journey had begun.

Intelligent planning had also begun. Based on Lachlan's skills, capacity and experience, planning had to be focused on the key areas critical to him achieving team selection in five years' time, 2016. This related to developing an intelligent training program, required to build technique, strength and speed endurance. He also required the right training environment with regards to culture, training partners, support coaches and financial support.

Finally, the most important aspect to achieving peak performance was having a 'performance mindset'. A performance mindset empowers athletes to design a personalised peak performance process, visualise peak performance and compete at peak performance when it counts.

In 2012, four years prior to the 2016 Olympics, Lachlan's strength was his raw speed and ability to race – both key areas required to compete at international competition – but these were not enough for him to succeed at international level. Lachlan had to focus on building his technique, team boat skills, and increase his endurance capacity.

It's all about the 'why'

In Lachlan's words this is how he approached training intelligently four years out from when he needed to peak at Rio in 2016:

When I had an endurance session, often 24 kilometres or two hours plus of paddling, I focused on performing every stroke technically correct. I had to have 100 per cent concentration. I wanted to improve each stroke. I wasn't out there to go fast or race anyone else. I was in my zone and no one else mattered. I knew 'why' I was doing this session some four years (1460 days) before Rio. I had clarity knowing that if I get it right today, then when it counts in Rio, my technique will hold together when under pressure with 250 metres to go and fatigue setting in.

Through intelligent training and asking the right 'why' questions, I would finish a session far more mentally exhausted, rather than just physically tired. I found mental exhaustion far more taxing; it is easy to just paddle 24 kilometres. I have witnessed competitors paddle 24 kilometres as hard as they possibly can. Flat out, physically spent. However, not for one second has thought been given as to why they are doing this session. Not one question has been considered relating to why or how this session will impact performance on the chosen day in Rio. They have only focused on the doing the 24 kilometres (the 'what') as hard as possible so they can tick the box, session done. My aim is when I line up to compete I have done the most amount of intelligent work, not simply the most amount of work.

That's how I see most competitors, just ticking boxes. Over time this results in stagnant or declining performances. When the focus is simply to train hard and tick boxes, you quickly roll from session to session, day to day, week to week, never really understanding the process required to deliver peak performance when it counts. Basically, there is a lack of learning, and this results in the athlete repeating the wrong behaviours that are contributing to a decline in performance.

ALWAYS LEARNING

What separates athletes and businesses owners who consistently perform at an elite level from everyone else? Elite performers in sport and business all learn from every performance. They review the process and identify what areas require improving – and, importantly, they apply the new process. This becomes a continuous cycle of learn, think, apply and so on.

As a business leader, your goal is to build a great business, with a great team, delivering great financial and lifestyle rewards. You cannot afford to make the mistake of being stuck on the job site with your team. You must get out of the 'just work hard' mentality. You must fully appreciate and understand the power of a scoreboard, the power of sharpening your saw, the power of observation, the power of trusting your team and the power of working intelligently. If you truly believe in this, you are on the pathway to success.

Your takeaways

1. Identify the areas in your business that require sharpening – do not mistake activity for productivity.

2. Develop your scoreboard to measure performance – business intelligence drives educated decision-making.

3. Before doing a task, ask yourself why you are doing it – don't get caught up simply ticking boxes.

CHAPTER 3

Not bringing your 'A-Game'

LEARN THE RULES OF THE GAME

Business is a game and to be successful you need to know the rules of the game. Throughout this book I make reference to a key rule in the game of business known as your 'A-Game'. In the game of business your A-Game is a critical factor in determining your success or failure. If you really want to build a great business that serves you in providing a great lifestyle, following the A-Game rule is non-negotiable. The rule is simple: you must bring your A-Game to everything you do. Most businesses fail due to the business owner's lack of quality and lack of detail when doing tasks.

A-Game relates to the level of focused energy and detail invested to complete a task. A-Game begins with you as the business owner. When you bring your A-Game to every task, your team will follow. And I mean every task, not every second task.

For me, A-Game is an important value I live by. I use this to sense check whether the task is worth doing or not. This check highlights if the task at hand will generate value for the team, my clients and my business. If I am not prepared to bring my A-Game to a task, it is not a priority, and so I push it aside.

What does A-Game look like? The following table compares the difference between Other-Games and A-Game through looking at the tasks the business owner must complete during the course of a job.

Task	Other-Games	A-Game
Create quote	• Limited to no review and research • No double-checking calculations • Complete last minute	• Complete review and research of scope, specifications, solution alternatives, deliverables • Triple-check calculations • Complete well before due date
Submit quote	• Email quote • Often delivered after the due date	• Call before due date to confirm quote will be sent on time • Ask to confirm the requirements of the quote submission • Arrange a meeting to confirm solutions meet the required scope • Hand deliver or email quote on time
Follow-up quote	• No follow up	• Call to ensure quote was received if emailed or posted • Conduct meeting to confirm solutions meet the required scope • Discuss potential alternative solutions

Task	Other-Games	A-Game
Prior to job commencement	• Very limited planning and no team meeting	• Detailed planning and preparation to confirm capacity and deployment of resources • Conduct team meeting to communicate job stage deliverables and timelines – setting clear expectations and accountability
Commence job	• No tracking of actual progress versus quoted • Client meetings are conducted on the run, ad-hoc	• Track actual progress against material and labour allowances for each stage • Conduct regular scheduled meetings with client throughout the job to confirm on scope
Complete job	• Delivers inconsistent results • Hit and miss with delivery • Often no money made from the job	• Delivers consistent results • On time and on scope • Client expectations exceeded • Profit targets achieved
Invoice job	• Often invoicing not processed until well after completion	• 100% of the time job invoiced at time of completion or milestone reached
Payment	• Terms and conditions often lacking critical detail and not signed prior to commencement of job • Variations managed ad-hoc	• Clear terms and conditions signed off prior to commencing the job • Clear process to manage variations

UNDERSTANDING THE IMPORTANCE OF A-GAME

Why is A-Game important? A-Game relates to the 1 percenters that most people do not think are important. When you are 100 per cent committed to operating in the business performance mindset, A-Game dictates where you choose to spend your time. Simply, if the task is not worth bringing your A-Game to, don't do it. You only have one game period: A-Game. The business performance mindset owner understands the negative impact if Other-Games are brought to a task. The negative impact is not instant, but usually felt over time.

For a tradie business owner operating with the tradie mindset syndrome, jumping in to complete a task is easier than stopping and asking why this task is important to the business. Rather than contemplate the A-Game approach of investing time on prioritising a task to-do list, their goal is to get as many tasks done so they can be ticked off the list. They then feel a great sense of achievement because things are getting done and boxes are ticked. Wrong.

Herein lies why mindset is the key to achieving greatness in your life. The tradie mindset syndrome lulls you into a sense of mediocrity because you do not have a large enough view of the world. This mindset only provides a snapshot of what is to come, relating to today, tomorrow, next week and, if you're lucky, next month. This snapshot doesn't provide a larger view of the potential long-term impact today's decisions will have.

The following table shows some of the potential negative impacts resulting from bringing Other-Games to the task.

If you want to build a great business that dominates your market, bringing your A-Game is non-negotiable – for the owner, team members, suppliers and partners. A-Game is the way we do it here. All success follows A-Game. What game you bring is your choice.

Business situation	Bring Other-Game to task	Long-term outcome
Lots of jobs coming in – need more staff	Hire fast – lack of recruitment planning, lack of training, lack of performance review	Select wrong candidate – poor fit for the business, need to fire, costing time and money
Quotes piling up	Just get the quote done and submit it – job incorrectly scoped with incorrect specifications, job incorrectly priced	Jobs lose money, waste of time – less money in the bank
No money in the bank	Go 'cap in hand' looking for any type of job – even if not profitable	Jobs lose money, waste of time – less money in the bank
Running late to client meeting	Due to poor planning and preparation have no time to notify client running late	Client goes to competitor due to lack of professionalism – need to source new clients, which costs time and money
Meeting with accountant	Attend the meeting with no plan and no planned questions relating to information required to make better business decisions – sit waiting for answers	Poor meeting outcome resulting in inadequate recommendations, which costs time and money

PARTNERS MUST BRING THEIR A-GAME TOO

To be successful in business, your partners must follow the rules of the game and also bring their A-Game. By 'partners' here I mean your suppliers, accountants, bookkeepers, financial advisors, insurance brokers, finance brokers, consultants, coaches – and the list goes on.

Too often I have seen businesses fail because partners didn't follow the rules. Too often these partners become lazy in bringing Other-Games to the table. Rather than seek to understand the real problem or research a better solution, they take the easy option of churning out the same information they provide to all their other customers. Too often, partners think it is acceptable to bring their Other-Game to the table because 'a tradie won't know any different'.

I have witnessed firsthand families losing their homes because partners provided the wrong recommendations. You must demand and expect all your partners to bring their A-Game. You are investing in them to deliver results. This is where, as a business owner, you must bring your A-Game when engaging prospective partners. You must ask great questions in relation to what past successes they have achieved with a business the same as yours. And you must ask how they will improve business performance, and how their A-Game will be delivered always.

From my own perspective, I need to have the best partners on board to ensure our vision is achieved. Our vision is to be the Olympic Champions at changing thinking and behaviour to improve tradie business performance. I need to know that my partners have the same vision, the same commitment to achieve this vision, and the same belief that we will achieve the vision.

I have partnered with Telstra, Reece and Burson because they have the same vision relating to improving their customer's overall business performance. Due to our visions being aligned, I was engaged to influence their customers' thinking and behaviour.

Your takeaways

1. If a task is not worth bringing your A-Game to, it's not worth doing at all.

2. What areas of your business require your immediate A-Game? Uncover the process and system refinements that will improve long-term performance outcomes.

3. Have all your partners signed up to the rules of the game? Remember – the only rule is to bring your A-Game.

CHAPTER 4

Not having focus

BURN THE BOATS

When Alexander the Great, the world's greatest empire builder, arrived on the shores of Persia, his Greek army was overwhelmingly outnumbered. Yet he gave the orders to his men to burn the boats. As their only means of retreat went up in flames, legend has it that Alexander turned to his men and said, 'We go home in Persian ships, or we die'. No doubt this act was based on another of his quoted strongly held beliefs: 'There is nothing impossible to him who will try.' What followed was an extraordinary victory over an army that was in many ways superior.

This is not the only time in history that leaders have burnt their boats when faced with insurmountable odds. Sun Tzu's *The Art of War* brings to light the logic behind the decisions of history's greatest conquerors to burn their boats at the risk of being killed in enemy hands. Quite simply, doing so eradicates any notion of retreat from the minds of their troops and commits them unwaveringly to the cause – victory. Defeat isn't an option at all.

Nothing is like burning your boats to focus your mind on the one thing: the cause. The one thing is success. There is no plan B. What individuals and teams can achieve when backed into a corner with no other option than to fight is extraordinary. With no option of turning back, they have clear focus and are hungry to win; everything is laid bare on the line for the cause.

For me, closing my plumbing business in 1997 to venture into study and the corporate world was the burning of my boats. I was committed. There was no turning back. Because I had no plan B, I had to make it work. I had to find my way. It was the single most exciting thing I had done in my life. It was at that very point things became quiet. All the external noise faded. All the previous distractions disappeared. I now had one mission, and it was very clear. I was only focused on the tasks, people and thinking that would assist my cause.

THE PROBLEM WITH JACK OF ALL TRADES BUSINESSES

One of the main reasons tradie businesses struggle prior to failing is that the owner has no clear understanding on what their mission or cause is. This was the reason my plumbing business struggled. When you're operating in the tradie mindset syndrome, you think you must hedge your bets, just in case. You try everything. The business becomes a jack of all trades doing a lot of different types of work, but nothing is done great. Everything is completed just okay. Just okay means the customer easily forgets the business, and it has no 'wow' factor. Just okay means the customer expects a cheap price, no expert. Just okay means the customer won't refer the business, and feels no trust.

Lacking a vision

Jack of all trades businesses don't have a mission or vision to be known as the experts at a specific work type or client type. In chapter 17 I discuss how becoming a master in knowing your clients' actual problem will set your business apart from your competitors. You can never become a master if you work for all different types of customers. Residential clients have different problems to that of commercial clients. Maintenance clients have different problems to that of construction clients.

Being controlled by fear

Owners of a jack of all trades business will never make the call to burn the boats due to fear. Fear that if they focus on a niche, the work will run out. Fear that if they focus, they might miss an opportunity. Fear that if they focus, they might not be good enough. Fear that if they focus and put it all on the line, they might fail. Overcoming this fear is the first step to building a great business that will serve the owner, as opposed to a jack of all trades business that enslaves the owner. Once this fear has been overcome, anything is possible.

ELITE FOCUS

Let's think elite sports performance – think how do Olympians burn their boats? As discussed in chapter 2, along with working with business owners in building performance-based businesses, I have also worked with athletes and sporting organisations to implement elite performance frameworks. I have had the great opportunity of mentoring multiple Olympic athletes, and assisting NRL head coach of the Rabbitohs, Michael Maguire, during 2014 when they broke a 43-year drought to claim the premiership.

It always disappoints me when I see an athlete or a team with great ability failing to reach their performance potential, and never achieving a high-level of success. Never winning games or races they should have won. All the while, athletes and teams with a lot less ability out-compete them at every play.

I always think this is such a wasted opportunity. But I also know this often comes with a lifetime of regret. Times when the individual will look into the mirror and ask the question, 'What if?' What if I had changed my environment or took it more seriously? Would the results have been different? The question continually runs through their minds, and especially every time they witness others celebrating the taste of success they missed out on.

Before they hand out the medals at an Olympic Games, every athlete must fight to earn their place on the team. Every aspiring athlete must focus every day, over a four-, six- or eight-year period to earn the right to call themselves an Olympian. I believe the difference between those who earn the right to call themselves an Olympian and those who miss out largely comes down to focus: the focus to overcome fear and burn their boats.

This is how aspiring Olympians burn their boats. This is how they back themselves into a corner with the only option to come out swinging. They climb a mountain top to shout out for all to hear:

In four years' time I will be going to the Olympic Games. This is my discipline (for example, swimming), and this is my event (for example, 200-metres freestyle). For the next four years I will be investing my time, energy and thinking toward one thing. My mission is to make the Olympic team and win the Gold medal. I am putting myself out there. I am willing to sacrifice. I am laying it all on the line. There is no plan B. There is no retreat. I either make the team or I miss out. I need a support team on the same mission as me. I understand that I am opening myself up to criticism from others who will judge me from afar. I will perform at my best every day. The result will take care of itself. I will live with no excuses. I will live with no regrets.

As a business owner and leader, if you want to build a business and a team to perform at a consistent, elite level, do not sit on the fence. Stake your claim and shout out your intentions. Burn your boats.

Put it all on the line. Instil razor sharp focus. Do not live with regret. There is no such thing as failure.

One last word from two of the world's most successful business-men. When Bill Gates first met Warren Buffett, their host at dinner, Gates's mother, asked everyone around the table to identify what they believed was the single most important factor in their success through life. Gates and Buffett gave the same one-word answer: Focus.

Your takeaways

1. Define your one thing – what field, service or technology do you want to be known as the expert in?

2. Now use all your energy to focus on becoming this expert in your chosen field. What do you need to do to overcome your fear?

CHAPTER 5

Avoiding change

CHANGE IS TOUGH – NOW GET ON WITH IT!

We all know making a change in your life is tough. Kicking bad habits is particularly hard. You may have read breaking bad habits only takes 21 days, also 28 days – no wait, it's actually 66 days – and on it goes. From my point of view, achieving change doesn't come down to a number of days; change comes down to desire. Change comes from the questions you ask yourself and, importantly, from how strongly you answer these questions. *How much do I really want to build an awesome business? How much am I truly willing to sacrifice to achieve my dreams? How hungry am I to create a life of abundance? Am I willing to burn my boats?* As successful college basketball coach Bobby Knight once said, 'The will to win is not nearly as important as the will to prepare to win. Everyone wants to win but not everyone wants to prepare to win.'

Be resilient and keep going

If you answered the preceding questions strongly in the affirmative to change, the true test comes the next morning – and the next week, the next month and the next year. Your response to this test comes down to your grit and persistence. Can you keep getting back up from the knocks, from all the doubters, and from your own self-doubt? Can you keep going when things are not going to plan? When things are taking longer than expected or when the finish line is not in sight?

When these kinds of tests appear, most people quit. At this point, most people think it is all too hard to change, and that all those people who said it couldn't be done were right. At this point most people think, *I am comfortable the way it is; I don't need to change.* And they convince themselves that it is okay not to chase their dream.

Change can be tough. Change can be scary. Change can push you out of your comfort zone. But change can also transform you as a person. When I looked in the mirror back in 1997 when my client and debt collector took me for $33,000, I knew I had to change to become better at business. I was also fearful of the change I knew I had to undertake.

Yes, I was hungry, but I was also scared of the unknown. That was when I realised I had to trust myself that closing my business to commence study and gain experience in the corporate world was the right decision – even though I didn't know where to start.

Once I had burned my boats, you can imagine the comments that came next – when I told my staff, my clients and my mates that I was moving on from plumbing to studying business. The basic response was, 'Jonesy what the ... are you doing?'

I burned my boats again 10 years later in 2007 when, after gaining business skills, knowledge and experience, I quit the corporate world to start my own consulting business. I was ready to bring all my learnings from study and corporate experience back into the tradie space. My goal was to share with all tradies the 'must-have' knowledge required to be great at business.

This must-have business knowledge, found in abundance within the corporate space where performance is paramount, was not shared at trade school – where getting the job done is paramount. I aimed to change that. So there I was in 2007 with my new business venture, limited resources, one client, a young family, two mortgages and a very simple mission: make it work.

THE STRUGGLE MAKES YOU STRONG

Throughout my story of change, I had to trust my gut instinct to keep pushing through at many points. Times when I was struggling to get through the university workload and when I struggled to pass subjects. Times when I struggled to get a start in the corporate world because I was perceived as a plumber, rather than the business person I was willing to become. Times when I struggled to understand how the world of corporate politics worked because, as a tradie my previous focus had been on getting the job done, so I wasn't prepared for all the bullshit that goes on in the corporate world. And times when I struggled to attract clients and even struggled to pay the bills.

This is when your grit and persistence will be tested. Looking back now, the struggles I faced throughout my career provided the most important lessons in my life. They made me a stronger, more resilient person. Today when I am making change, or when things seem too hard or I lack belief, I draw on those previous experiences to provide me with the confidence to push on. I can tell myself it is okay, because I have been in this situation before and have prevailed.

The following parts in this book detail, step by step, how you can make positive change to build a great business that delivers great profit and offers great lifestyle opportunities. However, a magic bullet doesn't exist. You have to apply focused effort to ensure change happens – it will not just happen. Things will take longer than expected and will be tougher than expected, because you have never done this before. You must believe in yourself. You must surround yourself with people who believe in you, and beware of the people who place their own fears onto you – asking, for example, what will happen if you fail. There is no such thing as failure if you have a go. The only failure is not starting.

World renowned motivational speaker Les Brown talks about the graveyard being the richest place on earth – because it is here that you will find all the hopes and dreams that were never fulfilled, the books that were never written, the songs that were never sung, the inventions that were never shared, the cures that were never discovered. All because someone was too afraid to take that first step to carry out their dream.

One last point to remember: you've likely heard the quote 'the definition of insanity is doing something over and over again and expecting a different result'. Widely attributed to Albert Einstein but more likely originating from the Narcotics Anonymous organisation in 1981, the main idea stands. If you're not happy with your current results, and therefore want better results, you need to change your thinking, activity and focus.

Now get on with it. Get started on your blueprint for success, first by mitigating the five mistakes limiting business performance as follows:

- operate in the 'business performance mindset'

- be prepared to work intelligently

- always bring your 'A-Game' to all tasks

- have razor sharp focus

- make change happen.

Your takeaways

1. The hardest step is the first step – get started now.

2. Be prepared for a fight – if you get knocked down, get back up.

3. Take small bites and chew fast.

PART II

Stage 1: Clarity

No single professional sporting team or aspiring Olympic champion athlete in the world operates without a plan. Every sporting team and world class athlete is very clear on what goals they want to achieve and, importantly, what they need to do to get there. Before the season starts, sporting organisations assemble the right teams to deliver a premiership. And at the start of every four-year cycle, Olympiad athletes are assembling the right support team to deliver a gold medal. They have 100 per cent clarity.

If every professional sporting organisation places massive importance on planning and clarity, why is it that most professional business owners place zero importance on planning and clarity? Why is it that most business owners start their 'season' (that is, their 12-month financial year) with no idea where they are heading?

In this part of the book I highlight why clarity and planning is of paramount importance to help you not only safely navigate through your business landscape to ensure survival, but also actually generate a desired financial reward for all your efforts just in operating the business. Does any sporting team or athlete commence their season journey with no idea what the reward will be at the end? None. No-one would be crazy enough to invest morning and night to training, day in, day out, and sacrificing personal time without clarity as to what the prize is. So why do business owners invest countless hours every day, week, month and year with no idea what the prize is?

From this point forward, you need to always have your eyes focused on the prized reward.

CHAPTER 6

Understanding the Blueprint for Success

THINK LONG TERM *NOT* SHORT TERM

As a business owner, leader or manager, you're seeking to improve performance to achieve great success. So, think about this: who do you trust to provide you with the right information, at the right time? What information, processes and systems do you require? Where do you start?

Answering these questions requires research in terms of what best suits your business at that very moment in time. If you get on the wrong horse, one that fails to deliver the win, then the business could struggle for years. Time is crucial. Business owners must look for a proven, tried and tested method that will deliver the desired results, rather than wasting time and money trying to reinvent the wheel.

My Blueprint for Success framework is designed to power up your tradie business. The framework provides the required foundations to build a long-term sustainable business, not a quick business fix. Your goal as a business owner is to build a business that thrives for the next 5, 10, 15 or more years, not simply survives. The foundations need to be strong enough to withstand the storms that hit all businesses at various times.

The framework is not simply about getting a lot of customers knocking on the door. I hear the same stories, time and time again, from tradies engaging in sales solutions designed to increase sales. Yes, a lot of customers come knocking on the door, and yes sales can increase. However, a lot of the time the customers who come knocking are the wrong type of customer. Usually they are the 'race to the bottom' type clients, who will ring around for the cheapest price. This can send a business to the wall through wasted time and money. Any short-term peaks in sales can be often followed by long-term troughs in cash flow.

Pricing at cost is not sustainable

Following the GFC in 2009, when work was in short supply, a lot of businesses were sent bankrupt through poor choice of customer. The logic at the time was that providing work at cost was better than not working at all. The problem, however, was that delivering work drains cash flow rapidly. The more work delivered at cost, the quicker the business will become insolvent.

Having the ability to increase sales doesn't guarantee success. In chapter 13 I take you through the concept of 'growing broke' – where an increase in sales and workload actually sends a business broke. At the time of winning a job the business owner may experience a feeling of relief through winning the work – relief that the team will be busy. However, this relief is short-lived, quickly disappearing once the cash is drained and the line of financial credit is maxed.

BUILDING A SUSTAINABLE BUSINESS, STEP BY STEP

As covered in the introduction to this book, the Blueprint for Success framework outlines the four stages, step by step, to building a great tradie business that will guarantee you can work less and earn more. I guarantee if you, as the business owner, follow the step-by-step process, you will be able to make educated business decisions. And I guarantee that if you make educated business decisions with real-time accurate data, your business will be positioned to achieve long-term sustainable success. Yes, guarantee.

Teach for a lifetime

When it comes to building great businesses that consistently perform at high levels, I have a firm belief. This belief is encapsulated in one of my favourite sayings: 'Give a man a fish, and you feed him for a day; teach him how to catch fish, and you feed him for a lifetime'. Rather than simply helping business owners perform better for a day, a week or a month, the Blueprint for Success framework is designed to teach business owners how to perform better for a lifetime. This is achieved through identifying how business is to be approached, and through educating why and how to score the business to accelerate success.

The Blueprint for Success framework builds the Clarity, Control, Confidence and Connection all business leaders require to be successful. The framework has four stages, outlined over the next four parts in this book, which are broken down into steps, concepts, content and business tools. Everything follows an instructive pattern. The pattern is designed to present a problem and a solution. Once you know the pattern, everything else comes easy.

In my business, the key tool that identifies the pattern, delivering Control and Confidence for business owners is the 'CUBE' business intelligence software. The CUBE highlights where to focus time and energy based on a pattern or trend and, importantly, instructs what to do as a matter of priority. Simply the CUBE ensures you're focused on the important tasks that deliver the business profit – as opposed to being stuck in the 'tradie mindset syndrome', where you have no focus so every task is urgent. The first stage is finding Clarity, which the following chapters focus on in detail.

Your takeaways

1. Think about what you need to start doing today to ensure your business is positioned for success in 3, 5, or 10 years' time.

2. Long-term success is based on your business having strong foundations to survive the storms.

3. Learn the business success pattern – understand the key performance drivers to accelerate your success.

CHAPTER 7

Planning for your business landscape

According to climbing experts, if you start with no climbing experience and you plan to successfully climb Mt Everest, the world's highest mountain, you're facing a 5- to 10-year project. This assumes that you want to become fit and skilled enough to climb the mountain responsibly, without becoming a danger to yourself or others. Success is then based on the level of planning and preparation you invest in developing the necessary capability required to navigate the elements.

The same applies when planning to build a successful business – you must understand the environment you intend to enter. A lot of businesses fail due to a lack of awareness relating to the severity of the business operating landscape. Many business owners I see are totally unprepared for the conditions that lay ahead as the business and the economy move through different cycles. This lack of preparation leads to poor decision-making, leading to often dangerous outcomes that jeopardise the sustainability of the business.

UNDERSTANDING THE 4 Cs OF THE BUSINESS LANDSCAPE

Let's look at today's business landscape – that is, the reality. To operate a successful business today you must first understand the landscape you are operating in. Once you begin to understand the landscape, you can begin to ask great 'survival' questions relating to planning. Great questions lead to great answers, required to assist the decision-making process. And educated decision-making is critical to successfully navigating through what I call the '4 Cs' of doing business. The 4 Cs refer to:

- competition
- customers
- compliance
- cloud.

These areas are covered in the following sections.

Competition is fierce

How can you stay *relevant* to your target customers? Lots of new businesses are entering your market on a daily basis, offering your target customers with lots of choice. Tradies who are part of gen Y or the millennials generation typically want to drive their own business now. They do not want to wait; they want to be in charge now. And tradies starting a new business face low barriers to entering the market. With the information age and access to online qualifications, getting started takes less time and less money than in the past.

However, due to the ease of starting a business, most new business owners are totally unprepared. Often these new tradie business owners are taken advantage of by seasoned customers, who drive the price down so low that the business owners grow broke.

The key in this environment is working out how you can cut through the noise of all the competition to remain relevant to your target customers. How can you differentiate from your competitors so that when your target customer has a problem to solve you are the first to be called?

Customers have high expectations

What are your target customers' *problems* that you must solve to become the expert? With information all around us, customers have easy access to information and knowledge that was not available a decade ago. Your customers can research all there is to know about the products and service that you deliver. And with 'do it yourself' building and renovation shows continuing to hit our screens, your customers can quickly assume to be the expert. These 'screen experts' will happily tell people what the best solution is, how long it should take, and what you should be charging. As customers become more educated, their expectations also increase.

You must understand that what is unique one day becomes the expected norm the next. This means that if you 'wow' a customer one day with exceptional service, that same level of service is expected the next time. If you fail to deliver the expected level of service, you can easily be forgotten.

The key in this environment is not to focus on what the customer actually wants done, but on identifying their underlying problems. These problems can relate to time, flexibility, communication, solution options, maintenance and so on. Using a broken hot water system as an example, thinking that the customer's only problem is simply getting the hot water back on is a potential mistake. The problem may also relate to the type of solution, flexibility around timing or ongoing running costs.

Today you must become an expert in your customers' actual problems. More importantly, you must communicate how you understand their actual problems, showing empathy. This allows your customer to see the real value in your solutions, because you understand the real problem. Problem experts become relevant, and not easily forgotten.

Compliance can suffocate business

Have you got the correct systems and support in place to reduce potential risk to your business? Business owners must consider the compliance required to do business. What is the potential time and money impact relating to changes in taxation structure, changes in work health and safety requirements, or changes in employment legislation?

Due to the complexity of doing business, having the right support partners providing the right recommendations is critical to ensure your business is sufficiently protected. You need to look to the long term and plan for worst-case scenarios to ensure your risk is limited.

Your support partners – including accountants, financial advisors, insurance brokers and HR consultants – being fully aware of the landscape you wish to enter is of paramount importance. They are responsible for ensuring you are aware of the potential pitfalls on the journey and how to guard against them. For example, if you plan to increase sales and the size of your team, your partners need to ensure you have the correct business structure in place that allows tax liabilities to be minimised as well as protect personal assets. You must also be aware of a potential increase in workers compensation liability, and the legislation outlawing 'sham contracting' relating to the overuse of sub-contractors.

The cloud can be confusing

How can you automate processes with software to move operations into the cloud, improving team and client engagement? Invoicing a job in the 1990s was pretty simple: you just used paper and pen. Today the choice is endless, creating confusion. While tasks such as job scheduling and invoicing can be completed in less time, with access to instant information everybody expects these jobs done now. All transactions are being undertaken in the cloud and automated as we move to a cashless society.

I see a vast number of businesses wasting time and money after having selected the wrong type of software for their business model – because they don't understand what software is best for their type of business. Selecting the right software operating system must be based on understanding your ideal clients' specific problems, and the specific solutions they require.

When selecting software to operate in the cloud, understanding the future development plans for the software and how the software integrates with other cloud-based platforms is important. In other words, as your business grows and demands change, you must ensure your software has the ability to adapt and grow with your future needs.

The problems caused by this landscape

Without a clear understanding of what lays ahead, operating within this landscape presents often fatal problems for most businesses.

These problems include:

- Wasting time and money investing in multiple operating platforms that are often not suited to the business and therefore not delivering the required outcomes. This includes systems relating to accounting, job management, quoting, and sales and marketing.

- Not being able to leverage the gold in the data because of incorrect system set up and inadequate team training. This means the information becomes meaningless data that makes no sense and can't be analysed and used – in other words, rubbish in leads to rubbish out. Often the data lacks detail due to the initial focus being only on doing the task quicker, not understanding the business better. The data also becomes redundant if information is housed in separate systems. (These are called 'silos' within your business.)

- Poor decision-making due to no initial thought given to the reporting and analysis of this data, resulting in no business intelligence. Without business intelligence, decisions are often based on emotional, kneejerk reactions. Decisions are made for the short term, based on what needs to be done now, with no thought given to the long-term vision. This results in a lack of understanding on where best to invest time, meaning urgent tasks always win over important tasks.

- Business becomes rudderless, moving fast but going around in circles due to a lack of clarity regarding the navigation. With a lack of integrated information systems that place all the pieces of the business together, the business is unable to analyse all sides of the business at once. I liken this to setting sail with only a compass to find the direct route – unless you're also analysing the tide chart, the weather forecast and what craft will best suit the prevailing conditions, you're courting disaster.

You will never change the landscape, so stop wasting your time talking about how tough it is. If you choose to enter this playing field, you must learn the rules of the game. Next, you must plan and prepare your strategy to enable you to win the game. Like climbing Mt Everest, operating a business is very risky, so you always have to have your eyes wide open to what lies ahead. Develop a plan, always be alert and always be on watch.

FAILING TO PLAN IS PLANNING TO FAIL

As a business owner, you are undertaking a risky expedition. Reaching your summit requires detailed planning and preparation. Global research into business failures consistently lists a lack of planning as one the main reasons, and this is no coincidence.

The tradie mindset syndrome pushes planning way down the to-do list, so planning never becomes a priority. You never have enough time as the owner because you're always busy doing the work. Therefore, you never get around to planning, and never understand what the real priority tasks are on the to-do list – those tasks that will ensure the business is positioned for future success. These tasks are the ones that will ensure you achieve your personal goals. Planning is required to keep prioritising these tasks.

Also note that a plan is only as good as its execution. I have seen many a great plan go to waste due to the owner not being able to prioritise the time to execute the plan. Having a plan is one thing; execution of the plan is the critical element required to achieve the plan. Failing to execute a plan is as bad as failing to plan in the first place.

Score Your Business:
How many business owners plan?

The Score Your Business assessment also asked trade service and construction business owners to assess the level of planning they had undertaken.

Business owners with a business plan

The number of participants in the assessment who did have a business plan, broken down by turnover, is shown in the following table.

Turnover	With a business plan	As % of category
Less than $300K	118	48%
$300K–$600K	46	41%
$600K–$1M	26	44%
More than $1M	26	52%
Total	216	46%

The key point to note there is that fewer than 50 per cent overall have a vision for their business in the future.

The assessment then asked about business owners' level of satisfaction relating to lifestyle, income, number of working hours and stress levels, based on having (or not having) a business plan. The following table shows the results from this question.

Turnover	With plan and satisfied achieving personal goals	No plan and satisfied achieving personal goals
Less than $300K	46%	26%
$300K–$600K	35%	17%
$600K–$1M	31%	12%
More than $1M	23%	8%
Total	39%	20%

The results in chapter 1 showed that only 26 per cent of business owners were satisfied their personal goals are being achieved. The findings here show 39 per cent of business owners with a business plan are satisfied – 19 per cent higher than business owners with no goal, with only 20 per cent of business owners satisfied.

The key point to note is that as a business grows in turnover, satisfaction drops markedly for owners without a business plan. Only 8% of owners without a business plan and with a turnover of more than $1,000,000 are satisfied. This highlights the fact if a business grows by chance and not by design, the owner is faced with the day-to-day stress of trying to safely navigate the business through unchartered waters.

Business owners with a three- to five-year goal

The assessment then asked business owners the following question: 'Do you have clearly defined three- to five-year goals? (Do you know what the business needs to deliver financially in order to achieve your personal goals?)'. Results from this question are shown in the following table.

Turnover	With a 3- to 5-year goal	As % of category
Less than $300K	54	22%
$300K–$600K	26	23%
$600K–$1M	15	25%
More than $1M	14	28%
Total	109	23%

Only 23 per cent of business owners have clear financial goals for the business. Most business owners had no goal relating to what the business needed to financially deliver to achieve their personal goals.

As previously, the assessment then looked at the level of owner satisfaction based on having a three- to five-year goal. The following table shows the responses.

Turnover	Goal and satisfied achieving personal goals	No goal and satisfied achieving personal goals
Less than $300K	50%	24%
$300K–$600K	50%	16%
$600K–$1M	53%	7%
More than $1M	50%	14%
Total	50%	19%

The key point here is the significant correlation between having a goal and satisfaction, with 50 per cent of business owners with financial goals being satisfied, well up on business owners with no goals, with only 19 per cent being satisfied.

These results highlight the fact that having a plan and setting financial goals leads to greater business owner satisfaction. The critical aspect is for all plans to be effectively implemented and all goals to be effectively measured.

Your takeaways

1. Understand the business landscape you intend to enter – ask great questions of your support partners to ensure great recommendations.

2. Develop your business plan – define a clear vision where you want to go.

3. Set your financial goals – what must the business deliver you financially to achieve your personal goals?

Case study:
Good things come to those who plan

People have a tendency to overestimate what they can achieve in the short term, and underestimate what they can achieve in the medium to long term. However, from experience, to achieve remarkable results can take time, often 2, 3, 5, 10 years. When you think how long it has taken you to get your business to where it is today this should not come as a surprise.

One such client who overestimated what he could achieve in the short term was Brad, who at the time was a one-man band operating a plumbing maintenance business. Brad had been struggling with the business for several years. We met with Brad in July 2014 to create a business plan designed to create a healthy financial return on his investment. When we presented the three-year performance plan Brad wasn't happy because he wanted to achieve a $150,000 financial return in one year, not three years. Brad wanted it now; he couldn't wait to get this result, or so he thought.

After some heated discussion with some home truths ringing true, Brad finally agreed to locking in the three-year profit plan. We then set about implementing the Blueprint for Success into Brad's business. Simple focus: say no to 'Mr Creature' clients, price was based on profit required, implement processes that will free up Brad from doing every task, and recruit a team that believed in 'the way we do it here' to follow the process.

The following table outlines the initial performance as it was operating in July 2014, the three-year planned performance to be targeted by July 2017 as agreed in July 2014, and then the actual performance achieved in July 2017. When we compared the 2017 actual performance with the 2017 plan and 2014 performance, Brad was blown away. Back in 2014 he never dreamed he could build a business that can operate without him while delivering a great financial return on investment. The years of pain and sacrifice have now been worth it.

Performance improvements from 2014 to 2017:

- Sales – increased by $849,000
- Brad's wage – increased by $40,000

- Operating profit – increased by $194,000

- Brad's total financial return on investment – increased by $234,000 (pre-tax).

I'm not saying it's easy to achieve a performance turnaround like this, and I am not saying Brad didn't work hard for the results, but what I am saying is this could be your business in three years' time. It's a journey, but the sooner you firstly plan and then execute the plan, the sooner you will be satisfied all your investment in time and money is being financially rewarded.

	Current performance as at year ending July 2014	Change was needed – in August 2014 a three-year plan was developed to achieve financial goals	Planned performance for year ending July 2017	Plan was executed – in July 2017 a fantastic result was delivered. One that could have never been imagined three years prior in 2014	Actual performance for year ending July 2017
Sales	$135,000		$560,000		$984,000
Team numbers	1		3		4
Owner wage	$40,000		$80,000		$80,000
Operating Profit (after owner draws wage)	–$2,000		$80,000		$192,000
Total owner financial return	$38,000		$160,000		$272,000

CHAPTER 8

Be clear on your accountability

DON'T BE A VICTIM

As a business owner you must be accountable. Successful people are accountable. Successful people own the situation, and focus on what they can control. Successful people understand that results depend on them, no-one else. To be successful in any endeavour you must be accountable for your actions and for your results.

When business owners approach me for help with improving their business performance – be it a plumber, builder, electrician or landscaper – they are often at a stage where they are ready to quit the business. They are done, over it. When I ask them why their business is underperforming, I usually receive the standard 'tradie mindset syndrome' response. I am told that competitors are pricing low and undercutting them, or that customers do not appreciate the value delivered. Or I am told the government is making running a business too hard, or that the internet just makes things more complex. I am told you cannot find any good tradesman.

All these excuses can be boiled down to one word: blame. This is a common 'victim' attitude response. Basically, what they are saying is their results are independent of their decision-making as the business owners. Their results are based on the business landscape that they have no control over. Let's stop right there.

Get over it. What I am waiting to hear when I ask why your business is underperforming is accountability. I want you, as the business owner, to face reality that you have created an underperforming business. What you are currently experiencing is based on all your previous decisions and lack of decisions. Moving forward, to improve business performance, you must improve first. Once you are truly ready to improve as an individual, you are ready to build a business by design, as opposed to by chance.

Accepting the reality

Here I'd like to share a story of a husband and wife team who had been operating their plumbing business for over 10 years. Let's call them Marcus and Jane. After attending one of my How to Power a Tradie Business workshops, they signed up to my Blueprint for Success program. Upon starting their first session, Marcus made a very clear first statement:

I am sick of dealing with f#@!wits who have no idea. Sick of wasting loads of time with customers who do not know what they want; they want everything for nothing, and in the end they don't pay. Personally, I cannot keep going on and I want to shut the business down.

Jane then stated:

For me, the issue is that for all the work and effort Marcus puts in, we are still behind financially. We cannot draw a regular wage from the business, we have huge personal debt that we cannot get away from, and we never get away with the family for holidays.

We are lucky to have a couple of days off over Christmas. I am still working part-time in my job because the business cannot afford to pay me a wage. To be honest, it is very frustrating living in a constant struggle.

Moving from blame to accountability

My response to this kind of situation is simple: stop blaming others for your circumstances. If you want to design a business and, ultimately, a life of choice, you must take ownership and accountability for your results. If you want to be a constant victim to the business environment, do yourself a favour and shut the business down. Go work for someone who will guarantee 52 weeks' pay, superannuation, four weeks' annual holiday, paid public holidays, sick leave, long service leave, and no mental anguish from having the business top of mind 24/7. Now your choice is clear: victim or accountability?

I am happy to say Marcus and Jane chose accountability. Through changing their mindset and applying the Blueprint for Success methodology and tools over an 18-month period, their fortunes have dramatically changed, with income increasing by 50 per cent. More importantly, operating profit has increased by 150 per cent. This was achieved by sacking time-wasting 'Mr Creature' clients (the ones who always ask for price reductions, are slow to pay and are constantly bargaining to try to get something for nothing – more on them in chapter 18). Marcus and Jane also increased prices based on value delivered, automated processes and had the confidence to make great business decisions.

So what did this mean from a personal perspective? They now have cash in the bank, meaning Jane can work in the business full-time, drawing a weekly wage. Marcus has a lot more time and is not constantly on the phone. He can now enjoy three weeks of uninterrupted holiday over Christmas – leading to happy kids, happy wife, happy husband, happy life.

Marcus and Jane's situation mirrors that of thousands of tradie business owners I have assisted over the past decade. When business owners are inflicted with the tradie mindset syndrome, success becomes reliant on everyone else. They have a total lack of control and, ultimately, are constantly fighting for survival while being enslaved to the job.

Live above the line

To build a great business that dominates your market, you and your team must all live 'above the line' (as shown in the following figure). If everyone lives above the line, the business will be known as progressive, innovative and continually striving to deliver their customer promise. This is the result of a culture of ownership.

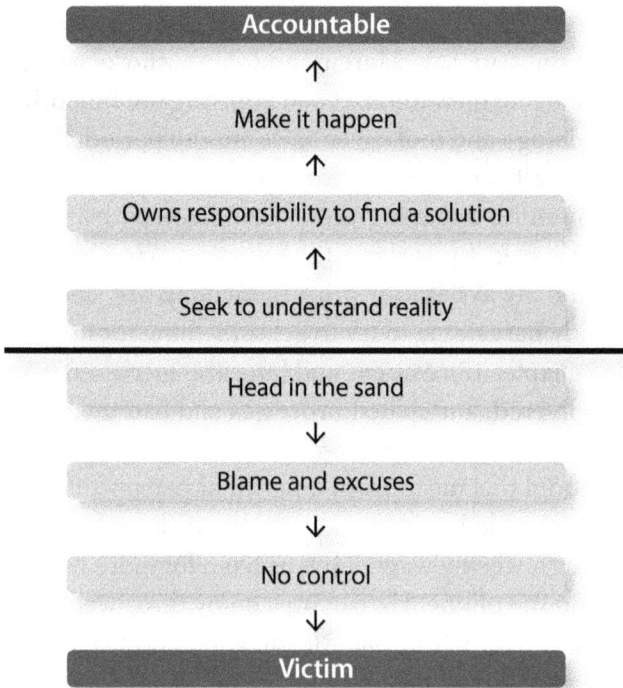

Accountable
↑
Make it happen
↑
Owns responsibility to find a solution
↑
Seek to understand reality

_____

Head in the sand
↓
Blame and excuses
↓
No control
↓
Victim

Over the years, I have personally conducted hundreds of individual performance reviews using various systems and methodology. For me, getting to the heart of an individual's attitude and whether they fit the culture of the organisation means judging their performance above or below the line. Individuals who cannot get above the line are not the right fit for that organisation. A simple discussion about parting ways now being better for everyone will need to be scheduled. (I discuss the importance of culture further in chapter 11, which looks at forming your 'way we do it here'.)

INCREASING YOUR ACCOUNTABILITY

The following sections provide some tips on increasing your own accountability – through paying attention to your locus of control and taking advantage of accountability groups or mentors.

Moving to an internal locus of control

'Locus of control' relates to accountability versus victim, because it outlines the extent to which people believe they have power over events in their lives. A person with an internal locus of control believes they can influence events and their outcomes – in other words, they have accountability. Someone with an external locus of control, on the other hand, blames outside forces for everything, and is always the victim.

Successful people take control of their lives through an internal locus of control. If you feel that you are powerless and you cannot control your life, do the following:

- *Listen to your thinking.* If the 'blame channel' or the 'excuse channel' plays repeatedly in your mind, you are shifting responsibility for your decisions – and, ultimately, your life – to others. Change channels, and eliminate blame and excuses.

- *Listen to yourself when you speak.* In your conversations, do you hear yourself blame others or blame the environment for things that don't go exactly as you want? Stop the conversation, think accountability, and talk about ownership.

Accountability groups and mentors to power up

A great way to drive accountability is to be part of accountability groups with like-minded business owners where you can share your goals and actions with the group. The group then holds you accountable to delivering on your promises in the agreed time lines. A coach or mentor can also assist in powering up your business performance. Every successful sportsperson and business person has behind them a coach holding them to account. Going it alone is very hard.

Ultimately, to ensure your dreams become reality you must be accountable. Do not rely on anyone else to make it happen for you.

Your takeaways

1. Your results are based on all your previous actions – both good and bad. You must face reality and accept responsibility for your current circumstance.

2. Ensure you and your team live above the line – be accountable and take ownership every day.

3. Seek out a mentor group that will make you accountable for your actions.

CHAPTER 9

Believe in yourself

KNOW YOUR BIG VISION AND AIM HIGH

In life, you have a choice. You can choose to aim high with a big vision and big dreams, or you can choose nothing at all.

Unfortunately, a lot of people never aim high with their dreams due to a fear of failure and rejection. Whether it be in personal, business, sport or study areas, people are constantly limiting their potential because they want to remain in their comfort zone. They never want to put themselves out there, to put it all on the line, to be exposed to failure. Therefore, they never dream, and they never have a vision of achieving much at all. They never imagine great things happening to them.

Have the courage to imagine it and speak it

I have had the great privilege – as a coach, mentor and sounding board to business owners and athletes – to witness people achieve great success that others thought was impossible. These same people started with doubt, fear and uncertainty. However, once they imagined their big vision, they could begin to see it. Once they had the courage to tell everyone about their big vision, they put it out there. Through 100 per cent belief and focused action, they followed through every day until it was achieved.

Your duty is to be successful

You are reading this book because you want to improve the performance of your business. You likely also want to improve your financial rewards for investing in your business and improve your overall lifestyle. As a business owner, you have a lot riding on the success of your business. Therefore, I believe that it is your duty to be successful.

A successful business all starts with your vision. If you are willing to have a go, make it big. Do not follow everyone else down the path of mediocrity. Don't base your goals and dreams on those around you, especially those who have aimed low all their lives. Don't limit yourself because your friends, family and colleagues have limiting beliefs.

This is very important. When people say you can't do it – or it's too hard, or you don't have the ability, aren't smart enough, or are too poor, too slow or too short – they're casting their own fears onto you. Brush it off and keep moving forward. Their fears are not yours. By communicating your dreams, you will quickly find out which people want to support your dream, and which people want to extinguish your dream. Be alert.

Are people laughing?

I have a simple test to assess whether a vision is big enough. With all my clients and in all my workshops, I state that if you communicate your vision to the world and if people do not laugh at it – do not question it or scoff at it – then it's not big enough. I simply mean that you want to chase a vision that most people could never imagine. You want to chase a dream worth investing in.

Why? Because as you move toward building a great business and a great life you are embarking on a journey of blood, sweat and tears, for years upon years. So you better make it a worthwhile investment by aiming high. But hear this: even if you aim low, you are still on a journey of blood, sweat and tears, but in this case towards mediocrity. It takes the same amount of energy and effort to operate a poorly performing business, so it makes sense to aim high from the start.

History shows that those people who were laughed at from the start usually end up having the last laugh. Plenty of individuals and organisations had their big dreams laughed at prior to achieving success. For example:

- When the Wright Brothers were trying to invent the first airplane, people laughed.

- When Gandhi attempted to create an independent India through non-violent means, people laughed. (He went on to say, 'First they ignore you, then they laugh at you, then they fight you, then you win.')

- When Bill Gates announced that one day every desktop would have a personal computer, people laughed.

- When Roger Bannister declared that he would run the mile in under four minutes, people laughed.

- When Alexander Graham Bell first invented the telephone, people laughed.

Make them laugh at you.

KEEP BELIEVING

When I was 14 years old and practically growing up at the Maroubra Surf Life Saving Club, my dream was to stand on the Australian medal dais for surf ski paddling and to represent Australia at the

Olympic Games in kayak paddling. People laughed at this dream. I wasn't a naturally gifted paddler. At the time, I was actually the slowest paddler in the club. I would go to competitions only to get knocked out first round. I continued to dream. I would do extra training sessions, yet my performances didn't improve. I continued to dream.

One day, five years later, I woke up and realised I needed to change my environment. I decided to move to where Australian champions and Olympic kayak paddlers trained. When I packed my car with all my worldly belongings, ready to leave Maroubra for the Gold Coast, some people laughed, saying that I would be back in six weeks. I continued to dream.

The only thing I had was the belief that I can achieve my dream. Belief kept me hungry. Belief kept me searching for new ways to improve my performance. If I had lost my belief, I would have settled for what I had been exposed to. Having belief forced me out of my comfort zone, and forced me to move to the Gold Coast with no plans.

Two years after moving to the Gold Coast, I realised a dream of standing on top of the dais as an Australian champion. What an unbelievable feeling of satisfaction. I was on cloud nine. I appreciated the journey of hard knocks I had travelled. I understood that all the hard times had prepared me for what lay ahead on the journey. If you are prepared to push through the hard times and learn from every experience, you become a stronger person. You become resilient.

After winning my first Australian championship, I was then fortunate to represent Australia in kayak paddling. Even though I failed to achieve my dream of representing Australia as an athlete at the Olympic Games, I have had the opportunity to coach Olympic medallists. I was also presented with a fantastic opportunity to commentate the 2016 Rio Olympic Games canoe and kayak events for Channel 7. All these opportunities were made possible because, as a 14 year old, I aimed high with a big vision, and I kept believing.

Success doesn't come without failure

JK Rowling, author of the *Harry Potter* series, spoke to the graduating class of Harvard in June 2008 – not about success, but about her failures. This is her great quote relating to failure.

> *You might never fail on the scale I did, but some failure in life is inevitable. It is impossible to live without failing at something, unless you live so cautiously that you might as well not have lived at all – in which case, you fail by default.*

She should know. JK Rowling didn't magically become astonishingly wealthy overnight. Her story is inspirational. While penniless, recently divorced and raising a child on her own, she wrote the first *Harry Potter* book, using an old manual typewriter. Twelve publishers rejected the manuscript. A year later she finally received a publishing green light from Barry Cunningham, then-publisher at Bloomsbury Children's Books, but he insisted she get a day job because he stated that there was no money in children's books. How wrong he was.

What if she'd stopped at the first rejection? What if she'd stopped at the second rejection? Or the tenth? A measure of success is how many times you keep moving forward despite hearing only no. Success never happens in a straight line and success doesn't happen without failures. That's reality.

YOUR VISION – START WITH THE END IN MIND

In *The 7 Habits of Highly Effective People*, Stephen Covey developed the habit of beginning with the end in mind. On his website, he talks about whether you are the person you want to be:

> *So, what do you want to be when you grow up? That question may appear a little trite, but think about it for a moment. Are you – right now – who you want to be, what you dreamed you'd be, doing*

what you always wanted to do? Be honest. Sometimes people find themselves achieving victories that are empty – successes that have come at the expense of things that were far more valuable to them. If your ladder is not leaning against the right wall, every step you take gets you to the wrong place faster.

Is your ladder leaning on the right wall?

Covey describes living a life worth living. Decide what is truly important to you, and take steps every day towards your vision, even though at times it may feel like you are going backwards. Think about what makes you happy. What are the things you are passionate about? This is the starting point for your vision.

With a clear vision of what you want to achieve, you can start to plan how to get there. Think of a block of dirt. The owner has a vision of how they would like to transform the patch of dirt into a family home that will hold lifelong happy memories. When you 'start with the end in mind', you begin to picture what the home will look like. Ideas start flowing relating to the structure and required feel of the home – two stories, four bedrooms, pool, entertainment area, big kitchen and, of course, a parents' retreat. A parents' retreat, that would be nice, wouldn't it?

Once you start with the end in mind, you realise you must find an architect who can see your vison. This can be a hard process – finding someone who is switched on to your way of thinking is not easy. Only when you find this person can you commence to design the home. With the blueprints and 3D imaging prepared, you begin to get a clear picture. With this clear picture of what your vision looks like, you can begin to source the right partners who will assist you in creating your vision – including your builder, tradies, engineers, certifiers, surveyors and interior designers.

Selecting the right partners is the most important part. However, having clarity relating to every detail of your vision makes the selection process easy. You are clear and confident with the skills, expertise and experience you require. Put simply, you do not want any builder. You want a team of partners who able to deliver your vision – perhaps they have before. They get it. They understand the potential problems well before the problem surfaces. They understand where you can save money. They understand how to make the process seamless, even enjoyable. Awesome.

Once the partners have been selected, construction begins. Where does construction start? The decision process is now simple. Construction starts with the foundations. The design of the foundations is based on the stability of the dirt and the size of the structure. Once foundations are laid, your partners can simply follow the plan – frame, roof, rough in, sheet, fit off, landscape, beer and wine.

For your own business think about this: how many times have you charged forward, making kneejerk and often emotional business decisions, without giving one thought to the end in mind. You give no thought to the design of the business you are actually trying to build. This is like laying a foundation that has been engineered to support a single-storey house, only to find out later you need to build a sky scraper on the foundations. I guarantee the building, and the business, will fall over. Likewise, constructing the roof before the frames are up is going to cause immense pain. This is not starting with the end in mind.

Coming back to accountability

Too many times I hear the tradie mindset syndrome talking when I ask business owners about their plan for the business. I ask them about their vison for the business, and their end game. The most common response is something along the lines of, 'I haven't got time to work on the plan. Right now I need to get the work done so I get paid,' or worse, 'I couldn't be bothered'.

I can tell you my prediction for a lack of vision. (It's similar to the great Mr T's response in the movie *Rocky III* when asked his prediction for his upcoming fight with Rocky – 'Prediction? PAIN'.) I know firsthand the pain caused through not having a clear vision. The pain that comes through 'win some; lose some', through constant financial struggle and making poor investment decisions. The pain from sleepless nights due to worry, lack of quality family time and not knowing if the business is actually moving forward.

Be accountable for your own business, outline your vision and plan, and avoid the pain.

BUILDING A GREAT SUPPORT TEAM IS NON-NEGOTIABLE

Please, if you only do one thing after reading this book, write down your vision and place it on the wall. Why? Because knowing your vision makes choosing who should be on your support team so much easier. Your support team have been there and done that before. They will determine your level of success or failure. As a business owner, your support team will include suppliers, legal advisors, accountants, insurance brokers, IT, consultants, coaches, marketing experts and bookkeepers. Your support team is critical to your business's success or failure.

Think about this: if you are a swimmer and you have a vision on your wall of winning an Olympic gold medal, you know you cannot settle for a second-rate support team. Your support team will need to include a swim coach, physio, strength and conditioning coach, nutritionist and yoga instructor, to name a few. You'd demand a great team who have guided others to Olympic glory. You'd demand that your support team works together, pulling in the one direction. You'd demand that everyone was on the same page, and that they bring their 'A-Game'. You'd demand improved performance every day, and you'd demand everyone to believe.

With a clear vision, your support team are alert, energised and pumped, knowing that every decision they make is critical to achieving the vision. Compare this to a swimmer who doesn't have a clear vision, yet is investing the same amount of time training as the swimmers with the clear vision of winning an Olympic gold medal. This swimmer is not thinking about building a great support team, and the lack of clear vision means the swimmer will settle for mediocrity, basing decisions on convenience rather than required skills and experience.

Never settle for mediocrity

The swimmer lacking in vision will settle for a support team that bring their 'Other-Game', who are often working against each other, pulling in separate directions. What is the end result for this swimmer with no clear vision? They fail to maximise their potential, resulting in missed opportunities. I have witnessed this hundreds of times – talented, keen, smart athletes who failed to reach their potential. Why? Because a lack of vision means you don't challenge or question those around you, you don't seek alternative solutions and, ultimately, you settle for mediocrity. A clear vision allows you to confidently articulate what it is you need, thereby attracting what you need. A big vision ensures you will never settle for second best.

Back to your business: when has a member of your support team let you down and failed to deliver on their promise? When a business support team member makes a wrong recommendation – either through laziness, lack of skills and experience, lack of professionalism, or all the above – your business viability and your personal wealth could be severely jeopardised.

Easily averted

I witnessed firsthand how the wrong recommendations from a support team wiped out a successful business – and, tragically, led to personal bankruptcy. After the GFC, I received a call from a husband and wife team who owned an air-conditioning installation business. The pair were totally stressed out. Their major client went bankrupt overnight with $250,000 owing. The bank overdraft was maxed, and the business was on life support. Their big problem was that their personal wealth was exposed to the business debt, because the business structure set up by their business advisory support team did not adequately protect the owners.

Over the course of the preceding 18 months, the business had been winning much larger contracts. The business support team failed to highlight that these larger projects increased their personal risk exposure. Given the fact the business was operating under a partnership structure, the business support team should have recommended the business move to a company trust structure. Due to a lack of basic insight and understanding, the owners where left stranded. After the GFC, work was limited and the owners were left with no way to trade out of the debt. Unfortunately, the business was liquidated, and the owners had to sell their personal place of residence to cover the debt. In the end, the stress of the situation led to the owners divorcing. Tragic.

GET CLEAR ON YOUR VISION

Having a clear vision from the outset allows your support team to recommend and implement the necessary business structure and systems. These will be designed to meet the needs of your business for today and well into the foreseeable future.

A clear vision clarifies what you need. A clear vision means you will not settle for mediocrity, providing you with the confidence to communicate your expectations to your support team. A clear vision allows you to design a life by choice, not by default. Failure will not be an option.

My big vision

My big vision is to ensure all construction and trade service business owners are successful in achieving personal, lifestyle and financial rewards. Our Blueprint for Success methodology and 'CUBE' business intelligence software aims to increase the level of professionalism throughout the industry to guarantee results. With automated business intelligence, the right decisions can be made well ahead of the required time. I see most business owners operating their business blind, which is like driving a car at night with no lights. The 'CUBE' business intelligence software alerts the driver that they are fast approaching a cliff – or that they're fast running out of cash when relating to business.

For my vision to be realised I require a support team who have already achieved great things. I require the best in software development, the best in IT, the best in financial management, the best in sales and marketing, and the best in customer communications. I've also focused on finding the best partners for my business, those that have the same vision of increasing the level of professionalism and business acumen within the industry. Through creating win–win relationships with national companies such as Reece, Telstra, and Burson, I can engage, inspire and influence large numbers of tradies in changing their thinking to improve their performance. If I don't invest the time and energy into building value into these partnership relationships, if I settle for mediocrity, or if I take the most convenient option, my vision will just remain a dream.

How far can your vision take you? I wrote this chapter of the book while sitting on a flight from Sydney to Perth, on my way to deliver our Blueprint for Success training workshop to tradie business owners on behalf of Reece and the Master Plumbers WA. I was excited to be able to meet people looking for help on how to increase the performance of their business through increasing profit and improving lifestyle. And I was excited to be able to change people's thinking and behaviours in a direction that will guarantee a great business, great financial rewards and a great lifestyle. For me, this was another step toward achieving my vision.

The following are examples of visions I have worked with clients to develop:

- Be known as the industry experts – the 'go-to' in the industry for the right advice

- Number 1 customer service – always delivering on our promise, wowing customers

- Change the way it is done – disrupt the industry with constant innovation to improve business performance and value delivered to clients

- Continual innovation to deliver customer satisfaction

- Develop industry leaders of tomorrow – be known for educating and inspiring team members to become great leaders through leadership pathways

- Contribute to the community through delivering disability access

Have a think about whether you can adapt any of these visions to create your own – or develop one from scratch. Either way, make sure you have perfect clarity on what your vision is and how you use this to choose your support team and start planning your business future.

Your takeaways

1. Develop your big vision with the end in mind – get excited and communicate it to all who will listen.

2. Based on your vision, select your support team of partners with a proven track record of assisting other similar businesses – do not settle for mediocrity on your team.

3. Even when things are not going to plan, keep believing.

Case study:
Reece and a win–win partnership

When I started Cube Performance in 2007, with a vision of assisting all trade service owners to build profitable, sustainable businesses, I knew I needed access to the market. Working with individual businesses, one at a time, was going to take more than my lifetime. I needed to leverage my time and my methodology. I needed to partner with an organisation that would value what I could offer.

My objective was to partner with a trade supplier that valued educating their customers in relation to business performance. And I wanted to partner with a supplier that positioned themselves as a business partner to tradies, not simply a supplier of boxes filled with widgets. I wanted to partner with a supplier that focused on providing their customers with a business solution, as opposed to simply providing materials at the cheapest price.

The only supplier that fitted this profile was Reece. From the initial discussions regarding the innovative concept, the message and the outcome, we were aligned with the same vision: to provide trade business owners (including plumbers, builders, landscapers and air-conditioning suppliers) with relevant, easy to understand business information and tools that would deliver business improvements immediately.

Reece clearly understood that by investing in their customers to help them operate their business more professionally and profitably, Reece would benefit. Through fostering long-term relationships, through customers having the cash in the bank to pay on time and, importantly, through assisting customers in profitably growing their business, Reece would benefit. For Reece, it was all about win–win.

The key for me was how the concept would be received in the field once the management team launched the program. From the outset, I was blown away by how the entire Reece team, from head office staff through to staff at all the branches across Australia, were on board with the program. All saw this as a great opportunity to add value to their customers' businesses. This is a credit to the 'way Reece do it', investing in their team to instil their core belief of customer satisfaction.

Since 2009, Blueprint for Success training workshops have been conducted throughout Australia – from Sydney to Perth, Hobart to Darwin, and Bendigo to Rockhampton, hundreds and hundreds of workshops have been conducted. Through the Reece partnership, I have had the opportunity to communicate with thousands and thousands of trade service business owners.

And when I revisit locations, nothing is better than a Reece team member or a tradie business owner who attended a training session years earlier shares their success stories with me. Business owners who were once enslaved to the job, battling survival on a daily basis, who since implementing the Blueprint for Success have now created businesses that serve them and their families through delivering profit and a lifestyle of choice.

These consistently positive results get me pumped and excited. This drives my passion and hunger to assist more business owners. For the tradie business owner, it solidifies their choice in choosing the right business partner in Reece. They now understand that their long-term business success depends on more than simply finding a supplier with the lowest price.

CHAPTER 10

Think profit *not* turnover

If you want to increase the money in your bank – if you want to understand what decisions you need to make to increase profit – you must first think profit not turnover. You must understand that profit is not a dirty word.

We always hear from a gambler when they win big. They are often quick to strut around, big-noting themselves on how smart they are at being able to pick a winner. Yet, we seldom hear anything from a gambler when they lose. The same can be said for some business owners. We hear about the big project won, often worth millions of dollars in turnover. However, we never hear if in fact they lost money on the project.

When I was operating my plumbing business, I would review construction plans to quote on the job. My first instinct was to have a quick glance through the plans to assess the size of the job. Once I had a feel for job size, I would then estimate the potential value or turnover the job could generate for the business. *This is potentially a $30k project, or $100k project, or $1m project*, I would think. *Awesome.*

I got caught up thinking about turnover from the outset, and based on thinking solely about this turnover, I started to think about what price would win the job.

Because I was fixated on the potential turnover and size of the job, I became short-sighted. I would feel relieved because the job was a potential solution to my short-term problems. I was thinking, *Great, I have enough work to keep the boys busy. Great, the pressure will be off me having to find new work for a while.*

The problem, however, when thinking only about turnover is that you give little consideration to the actual profit the project will deliver the business. I gave no thought to the required investment – in time, money, resources and, importantly, mental energy – to deliver the project. And I gave no thought to the potential long-term problems that undertaking the project would create for the business. This included placing pressure on all resources, including cash, team and systems.

BEGIN WITH FINANCIAL REWARD IN MIND

With financial reward, I'm not referring to a wage. I would like to confirm our terminology relating to financial reward. In the context of this book, the financial reward is the profit the business owner pockets after company tax. The financial reward is received after the business owner has claimed a wage for undertaking their role *within* the business. The financial reward is determined by how well the business owner has worked *on* the business.

When it comes to gaining clarity around what you want the business to achieve in, say, the next 6, 12 or 24 months' time, stating turnover as a goal is very easy. Throwing out some required revenue or turnover numbers doesn't take too much time or effort. Aiming for $500,000 turnover – or $10,000,000 turnover – is easy. The logical thinking at the time is that it sounds like a good number, so let's aim for it. Don't be fooled into thinking that a big turnover goal is good for your business. I see businesses turning over millions of dollars in revenue, only to be losing money. (I discuss this further in chapter 13, where I cover the concept of 'growing broke'.)

When I discuss a business owner's financial goal or reward, I always ask the simple question: what is the desired financial return on your investment that makes operating the business worthwhile? This is often met with a blank stare, or at best a confused answer relating to how much they want to take home each week. Let's be clear: if the goal of operating a business is to solely generate a wage, the business will not stay open very long. I recommend you go and work for someone else to save all the pain.

The financial reward for operating your business needs to be more than just to pay your personal expenses. Your financial reward should be big and juicy – a reward that will get you pumped up, even when you are having a tough day. Think about some great rewards that will make it all worthwhile, and that allow your family to appreciate why you are investing your heart and soul into the business. What if your business was a vehicle that enabled you to pay off your home mortgage in half the time, or enabled you to take the family around the world, or to take time off when you wanted to follow your passion? Now it gets interesting.

Importantly, you have a choice. You can choose to go into business for yourself, or you can choose to work for someone else. If you choose to go into business for yourself, you have more choices. You can operate a plumbing business, for example, or choose to operate a pub. If you choose to operate your own business, you must consider what a worthwhile financial return is for you. What is the business worth when taking into consideration all the countless hours you will need to invest into it? Think about all the time you will spend away from your family, all the sleepless nights worrying about no money in the bank and, finally, all the risk you are potentially exposing you and your family while operating your business. You must work out what this is valued at.

CHOOSE THE BUSINESS PERFORMANCE MINDSET APPROACH

As discussed in previous chapters, your operating mindset dictates your thinking, your thinking dictates your actions, and your actions dictate your results. If you are operating in the tradie mindset syndrome, you're thinking job and wage, and your actions dictate you are focused on the short term and keeping things ticking over. Results reflect a 'boom and bust' cycle.

Operating in a business performance mindset, on the other hand, you are thinking asset creation and return on investment. Your actions dictate you are focused on positioning the business for future success, and your results reflect sustainable success.

Operating in a business performance mindset, you expect a return for every dollar invested. If you invest $1, you expect to receive $2, $4, $8, $16 (or more) in return. You are always searching for and innovating new ways to improve the performance of each $1 invested.

Operating in a business performance mindset, you are fully aware of the opportunity cost relating to your investment. What are the alternatives where your time, resources and energy could be invested? What alternatives will generate a greater financial return, not just in the short term but in the long term as well?

In this mindset, you know it is not about the job; it is about the business. It is not about a wage; it is about a financial return based on investment.

Profit prediction provides your return on investment

Before the business season (your financial year) has started, you must calculate your desired financial result. You can call this your budget, goal, target, projection or forecast. Here, I refer to it as your prediction. Why 'prediction'? Because if you regularly report, review and manage the performance levers that are discussed in this section, you can predict your outcome. This is a shift away from the approach of most business owners – who only look at the results after the season has been completed. Once the season is over, however, it's too late to change anything. You can't change the result once the game or season is over. However, you can have an impact on the result during the season.

After examining your business landscape (your 4Cs – competition, customer, compliance and cloud – as covered in chapter 7), and after calculating a realistic financial target, it is decision time. It is 'Go or No Go' time. This means you can choose 'Go' – yes, it is an exciting target that will ensure I push through the tough times because the return is worth it. Or you can choose 'No Go' – no, the target is not exciting and clearly not worth the effort. This is when you begin thinking about opportunity cost, and the alternatives that could provide a greater return on your investment. You could also consider potential ways to alter your business model.

Stop right there. I know what you are thinking. I have heard something like the following over thousand times: 'I cannot forecast my sales or business for the next 12 months; I don't even know what will happen next week.' This is your tradie mindset syndrome talking. What you're really saying is, 'This is too hard, I don't know how, I haven't got time.' Here we go again. The great thing now is that you can check yourself relating to what mindset you are operating in. If you find yourself back in the tradie mindset syndrome, that's okay – just jump back into the business performance mindset.

Don't be scared, just believe

Remember the Marcus and Jane story we discussed in chapter 8? When I worked through the 'CUBE' business intelligence software platform with them to predict profit outcomes, they laughed at the numbers. We had predicted an increase in sales by $50,000 and an increase in operating profit by $95,000 on the previous year. They thought, after 10 years of making no money, there was no way this could be possible. I shook them around, and set the profit performance levers and accountabilities. Importantly, I instilled the belief and confidence that the prediction would be achieved.

As the business season got underway, we measured performance every month. Just like a sports team reviewing their performance after each game, we reviewed the business's vital stats. We measured our actual performance against the prediction, looking at what was good and bad, and where we needed to focus our energy on improvement. When we got to the end of the season, Marcus and Jane couldn't believe the 12-month performance results. The sales result was just $5,000 under prediction, and the operating profit was $9,000 above prediction.

They couldn't believe it; they were blown away. They asked how it could have happened. I explained it was simple: they had clear profit performance levers and targets to focus on each day, week and month. By doing the little things, or the 1 percenters, they were focused and working intelligently, and they were disciplined. They made it happen every day. Remember – it is not the big plays that win the game; it is all the little plays added together that make the big difference.

SEPARATE WAGE FROM FINANCIAL RETURN WITH DISCIPLINE

A simple way to get clarity relating to your financial return is to calculate your required weekly wage, and separate this from your desired financial return as the business owner. First let's look at your required weekly wage. You're paid your wage for doing the job, for turning up and putting the tool belt on, for hiring and firing staff, and for dealing with customers and suppliers. If you didn't do this work, you would have to hire someone else to do it. Remember

– you can earn a guaranteed wage working for someone else, without the risk and sleepless nights. The weekly wage is what you need to personally live off and pay the household expenses.

All our clients complete a personal cash flow forecaster to calculate their 12-month personal cash requirements. Based on this calculation, we can determine an appropriate weekly wage figure. This then becomes their personal budget that, with discipline, they can stick to by living within their means. All too commonly, business owners overspend on their personal lives, which then affects the business because they need to draw funds. Using the business as a 'petty cash tin' to support your personal life is a sure-fire way to drain cash from the business, increasing the risk of failure.

Your financial return for operating the business, as already discussed, is not your wage. Your financial return is based on what you draw from the business after all liabilities (including tax) have been paid. This is called your 'retained earnings'. I recommend that retained earnings are distributed to owners after the financial year, once all transactions for the year have been reconciled. Too often I see owners draw a dividend from the business prior to the accounts being reconciled, often leaving the business short on cash when all liabilities are accounted for.

USING FINANCIAL INTELLIGENCE TO KNOW YOUR NUMBERS

Having the ability to access accurate, up-to-date and detailed financial and customer information is the first step towards creating your 12-month profit prediction. Lots of business tools and spreadsheets are available and you can use these to input your data to create your prediction. We use our CUBE business intelligence software platform to allow me and my clients to follow simple yet detailed methodology to predict financial return on investment.

To commence developing your 12-month profit prediction you must invest time in digging down into your business to forecast what will happen in the following areas:

- sales revenue – broken down by work type, number of jobs, turnover, hourly rates and call-out fees

- cost of sale (your direct costs incurred to deliver your service) – broken down by materials, sub-contractors and so on

- cost of sale margins – per work type.

The following table provides an example of the information required to develop your sales revenue and gross profit predictions:

Work type (income stream)	Construction	Maintenance	Service work
Monthly number of invoices/jobs	5	20	15
Monthly turnover	$30,000	$30,000	$20,000
Hourly rate	$80	$100	$120
Call-out fee	–	$100	–
Monthly material expense	$10,000	$5,000	$5,000
Material margin %	20%	30%	30%
Monthly sub-contractor expense	$5,000	–	–
Sub-contractor margin %	20%	0%	0%

Once your sales revenue and gross profit predictions have been agreed, you then need to consider what level of investment is required to deliver these results. First look at the level of required overhead investment – broken down by categories, including team members (the owner, tradies and administration), office, equipment, motor vehicles, human resources, marketing and professional services.

The information in the following table then provides your 12-month profit prediction. This is the time to analyse your business model, assess the landscape, and seek advice from your trusted support partners to make a 'Go or No Go' decision with the plan. In the example shown in the following table, the business owner's planned financial return on investment, labelled as 'Operating profit (before tax)', is $191,323. Note this is after the owner has already allocated drawing a wage within the direct labour investment category.

Income	Annual total	Business KPIs – % of turnover
Construction	$330,000	33.5%
Maintenance	$375,000	38.1%
Service work	$280,000	28.4%
Total income	**$985,000**	100.0%
Gross profit		
Construction	$165,000	50.0%
Maintenance	$312,500	83.3%
Service work	$210,000	75.0%
Total gross profit	**$687,500**	**69.8%**
Investment		% of turnover
Direct labour	$274,349	27.9%
Management and admin labour	$154,829	15.7%
Office	$7,000	0.7%
Motor vehicle	$20,000	2.0%
Equipment	$12,000	1.2%

Investment		% of turnover
Human resource	$4,000	0.4%
Marketing	$12,000	1.2%
Professional services	$12,000	1.2%
Total expenses	**$496,178**	**50.4%**
Operating profit (before tax)	**$191,323**	**19.4%**
Operating profit margin %	19.4%	
Break-even sales	$710,887	

Once the plan has been signed off, you need to identify the key profit performance levers that will ensure the predicted profit is delivered in 12 months' time. The profit performance levers shown in the following table require measurement on a daily, weekly and monthly basis to guarantee the planned financial return on investment is achieved.

Sales target	Weekly target
Construction	$6,346
Maintenance	$7,211
Service work	$5,384
Gross profit margin %	
Construction	50.0%
Maintenance	83.3%
Service work	75.0%
Labour investment relative to income %	
Direct labour	27.8%
Management and admin labour	15.7%

The profit performance levers deliver clarity in relation to what needs to be measured and what needs to be achieved each week. This new-found clarity enables tasks to be prioritised based on what needs to be achieved for the week. Some of the priority processes and tasks requiring implementation include focused business development activity to deliver the weekly sales at the required gross profit margins, detailed quoting systems to ensure accurate pricing, and detailed job planning and scheduling to ensure the team is achieving required billable hours.

All this clarity comes from the financial and business intelligence delivered from knowing, measuring and reviewing your numbers. This is the key area in building your Blueprint for Success. No tricks, no magic pills, no big wins are present when it comes to delivering consistent profitable results. Stay focused on doing the little things great, every day. (For more detail in this area, also see chapter 15.)

Your takeaways

1. Your focus is not about the job and drawing a wage – it is about the business delivering a financial return on your investment.

2. Create your 12-month profit prediction plan – sign off on a clear financial goal.

3. Define your required profit performance levers – these are the key areas that must be measured to ensure your plan is achieved.

CHAPTER 11

Know the 'way we do it here'

YOUR OPERATING DNA

The 'way we do it here' is a statement that clearly communicates what you and your business stand for. The 'way we do it here' relates to your values, beliefs and purpose, and to your overall business vision. This statement captures the unseen, the intangible. It is who you are; it is in your blood and your operating DNA. This is how everyone associated with the business must operate. This statement describes how the business ticks, and it dictates daily habits and rhythm. It dictates where you choose to spend your time. The 'way we do it here' is non-negotiable.

It is my 100 per cent firm belief and passion that, to create a business of true value and meaning, one that dominates the market, serving the owners and delivering great lifestyle rewards, you must nail the 'way we do it here'. This is the desired culture for your business. Put simply, this states, 'If you want to be associated with our company, this is how we roll, period.' This applies to everyone, including owners, service partners, team members, clients and suppliers.

Be extraordinary, not ordinary

If you want to dominate your market, and if you want to attract great clients, team members and partners, then make a statement. Make a loud and clear statement. Make it known that you are different from every other beast in the jungle. Make it known who you are and what you expect. When someone comes to you and says something like, 'I have worked for a business like this before', without blinking you state, 'No, you haven't because there isn't another beast like this.' Be proud of who you are.

I have asked thousands of businesses owners the simple question, 'What is the way you do it here?' Unfortunately, 99 per cent of owners don't know. Or they respond along very general lines, such as 'We provide great service', 'We get the job done right the first time' or 'We have the best equipment, and we keep the trucks clean'. All of which are valid responses; however, these owners are really missing the heart of what their business really stands for. These statements are missing why the entire team must bring their 'A-Game'. They are missing why the entire team must be accountable in taking ownership of all situations, and why the business is different from every other business navigating the same landscape.

The lives of owners lacking a clear 'way we do it here' resemble the hamster on the wheel. They are constantly struggling to attract and retain great talent due to being ordinary, not extraordinary. At the hint of a better offer, talent will go to another job. These owners are constantly struggling to attract and retain great customers due to their failure to consistently deliver on promise. At the hint of a cheaper price, customers will shop elsewhere. These owners are also constantly struggling to find great support partners who can provide the right advice and business solutions. Unfortunately, time and money is wasted following poor recommendations. And these owners are constantly trying to manage cash flow to cover the bills.

At this point, a lot of business owners throw their arms up in the air and state it is all too hard, the business is not worth the hassles. With the tradie mindset syndrome in full swing, excuses and blame are given as reasons the business is struggling. The victim mentality has set in.

In the game or in the stand

The reason a lot of business owners become frustrated with operating their business is due to the feeling that to get things done right they must do them all themselves. They are frustrated because they don't feel supported by the team, or feel like the team are just not getting it. They feel even simple instructions need to be repeated over and over again, and feel like they need to constantly pull the team along.

I liken this to a game of football where the coach must jump the fence and onto the field to drive the attack as well as muster the defence, while the players are in the stands cheering the coach on. The coach is in the game, constantly scrambling to compete in every play. Everything is urgent at this stage because every play could be the difference between winning and losing. The team, on the other hand, have no sense of urgency because they can sit back cheering on the coach; in fact, the team do not even know the rules of the game.

Herein lies the problem: the team have never been instructed on the rules of the game. Because the team do not know the rules, they must rely on the coach to constantly jump in to take control while they can sit back and watch the game unfold. The team witness the coach running around in circles, yet do not understand what they are trying to achieve. And the coach, or business owner, questions why they are paying their team at all and what value are the team producing. Maybe it is time to give up the game.

Business performance mindset demands the business owner clearly defines the rules and then educates all team members on these rules. Business performance mindset owners understand that creating a successful game requires rules that allow them to be removed from the game all together. The owner must be in the stand, observing the plays to ensure all team members are in the game.

To play the game, you must follow the rules. To be in the game, you must follow the rules. To be part of the team, you must follow the rules. And to have fun, you still must follow the rules.

IT'S NOT PERSONAL – IT'S WHAT WE BELIEVE

Your number one priority as a business leader is to attract great team members, great support partners, great customers and great suppliers. To consistently attract great, you must understand why it is you do what you do – in other words, to create and communicate your 'way we do it here'. This statement is not about personality or emotion; it is about belief, heart and soul. These are the rules of your game.

The following sections take you through how you can create your 'way we do it here'.

Start with your values (your everyday behaviours)

Your values are you, your heart and soul. They are your moral compass. Your values will drive everyday behaviours. Your values will dictate all decision-making for every team member. Your values clearly state expectations for all to follow – no exceptions, including the owner.

Here are some examples of values:

- Always own the problem – find a solution
- Always place the team and customer before self
- Always deliver on your promise.

An example of these kinds of values comes from Tony Hsieh, CEO of the online shoe and clothing shop Zappos, who stated, 'To make customers happy, we have to make sure our employees are happy first.'

Let's consider the story of Jack, which, in this first part of the story, shows how strong values drive behaviour onsite. It is Friday 4.30 pm, Jack has just finished his last plumbing job for the day and is heading back to the Best Plumbing factory. This is Jack's last day before going on annual leave for two weeks. His travel buddies had planned to leave at 5 pm, and they have already started to call him, asking if he is ready to go. When he arrives at the factory, no-one is there – everyone has packed up for the day. Right now, Jack has a decision to make. He can decide to quickly dump the truck at the factory and get out of there so he can catch up with his mates. Or he can decide to follow 'the way we do it here'.

Even though he is under pressure from his buddies to leave immediately, Jack knows he has made a commitment to the team. Jack knows everyone on the team buys into what 'the way we do it here' means. For Jack, this makes his decision easy. He chooses to clean the truck, and to organise all tools and materials into the correct storage. He chooses to complete all the job details in the job card for all jobs completed. And he chooses to send an email to the owner and the accounts team updating his timesheet and any relevant work in progress information.

Why does he do this, even while no-one is looking? Because he is committed to the values. He committed to owning the problem of running late. This was his problem and no-one else's.

He committed to placing the team and customer first, because he knew it was his responsibility to ensure that the truck was 100 per cent ready for his team mate to use on Monday morning. Finally, he committed to delivering on his promise of completing the job cards and timesheets. For Jack, the decision was easy because he never wants to let the team down. Why? Because that is the 'way we do it here'.

Articulate your purpose (your customer promise)

Your purpose is why the business exists. Your purpose relates to the value you deliver to your defined market and client, and is your promise to the customer. Your promise states your intentions, providing your client with clear expectations. This is big, because in effect this becomes your guarantee. The team must deliver this promise. The team must own this promise. Teams that buy into the purpose are driven to deliver the customer promise – no matter what.

Here are some examples of purpose showing strong customer promises:

- Offer best solutions – for the short and long term
- Wow customers with exceptional service

Let's have another look at Jack. This time, it's 6 o'clock Monday morning and Jack's alarm has just sounded. Jack returned from his holidays with his mates late last night. After two weeks of fun, late nights and little sleep, Jack is hit with reality – and he's struggling big time. He just didn't want to get out of bed. He wants to hit the snooze button. Where Jack worked as a plumber previously, hitting the snooze button wouldn't have been a problem. It was usual practice to rock in 15 minutes late, take your time sipping your coffee, and skim the paper before cracking into the work. But not now. Not at Best Plumbing.

The 'way it is done here', at Best Plumbing, is that to be considered 'on time', you need to be 10 minutes early. For a 7.00 am start, for example, to be on time, you need to arrive at 6.50 am, ready to go. Jack knows this, he believes in this, and he owns this. He knows everyone owns it, and he doesn't want to let anyone down. No sleep, hangover, personal issues – doesn't matter. Jack knows he must bring his 'A-Game' when he crosses the white line. When he turns up, he knows his purpose. He knows the promise he must deliver to his team and to his clients. So he gets up and delivers.

Add your big vision (what you want to be known as)

We discussed the importance of having a big vision and aiming high in chapter 9. A key point I mentioned there and what I want you to understand again here is that regardless of whether you aim high or aim low, you will be investing blood, sweat and tears. The only difference is where you focus. With a low aim, you are focused on activity not direction. With a high aim, you are focused on productivity and clear direction. Often the same time is invested, the same money is invested, and the same risk exposure is undertaken. However, one option has you spinning on the wheel going nowhere, while the other is moving you forward.

Make it big, make a statement, make it a challenge, and have a massive go. An example of a vision is 'Be known as the industry experts and leaders – the key people of influence shaping how the industry operates.'

Back to an earlier part in Jack's story – where he gets inspired. Prior to Jack working at Best Plumbing, he was not satisfied with his previous employment experiences. He was always keen to work hard, and to go above and beyond to satisfy the customer. However, he would get shot down by others in the business trying to pull him down to their mediocre level. See, if Jack was bringing his 'A-Game' every day, it would make his teammates look bad. It would make them have to work hard, and they didn't want that because they are happy coasting through life. They are happy sitting on the fence taking pot shots at those having a red-hot crack at life. His previous employers had lacked vision and lacked inspiration, and this attracted individuals who personally lacked vision and inspiration.

Jack knew he didn't fit in and he needed a change. One day he bumped into an old mate who he went to trade school with 10 years earlier. His mate told him he worked at a place that inspired him to improve his performance every day. Their vision was to develop the best plumbers and individual leaders in the country. He also mentioned that a vacancy existed for the right type of person who was willing to continually learn and improve. Wow. Jack was attracted to this. Jack was in.

WHEN EVERYONE DOES IT, IT'S EASY

Once you've determined your 'way we do it here', you need to create your symbol to reinforce your belief daily. Your symbol could be a poster on your wall or a laminated A4 piece of paper stating your 'way we do it here'. The symbol needs to be used at tool box talks to share stories – both good and bad. Stories help individuals learn, bringing your desired culture to life. Your symbol should be the most worn-out piece of paper in the business, used to ensure everyone is on the right bus. When everyone is playing the same game, following the same rules, it becomes fun. It is always easy when everyone is doing it; this way, it becomes non-negotiable.

Just like attracting team members with the same belief, attracting support and service partners with the same belief is also critical. Your partners must believe in your 'way we do it here'. To ensure expectations are clear, I recommend providing all partners with a symbol to educate your beliefs and non-negotiables. No grey area exists, just the 'way we do it here'.

The following symbol shows how the 'way we do it here' could be summed up in a poster or handout for all to see and refer to on a daily basis:

The Way We Do It Here!

1. Our Values – Everyday Behaviours

- ☑ Always own the problem – find a solution
- ☑ Always place the team and customer before self
- ☑ Always deliver on your promise

2. Our Purpose – Customer Promise

- ☑ Offer best solutions delivering peace of mind – for short and long term

3. Our Vision – What We Want to be Known For

- ☑ Developing industry leaders – the key people of influence shaping how the industry operates

Score Your Business:
How many business owners have an induction and training program?

The 'Score Your Business' assessment also asked the 466 trade service and construction business owners about the level of team induction and training undertaken.

Business owners with a team induction and training process

The assessment asked owners the following question: 'Do you have an induction or training process for all new team members? (Provide job descriptions detailing your requirements and expectations, how performance will be measured)'. The responses are shown in the following table.

Turnover	With an induction and training process	As % of category
Less than $300K	27	11%
$300K–$600K	27	24%
$600K–$1M	12	20%
More than $1M	21	42%
Total	87	19%

The key point here is that only 19 per cent of businesses owners have invested in a process to effectively train and educate team members that clearly communicates the expectation of the role. This increases to 42 per cent of businesses with a turnover greater than $1,000,000 (who employ a greater number of team members).

The assessment then looked at the level of satisfaction based on having a team induction and training process. The following table outlines the responses.

Turnover	With an induction and training process and satisfied achieving personal goals	No induction and training process and satisfied achieving personal goals
Less than $300K	33%	22%
$300K–$600K	30%	17%
$600K–$1M	25%	29%
More than $1M	24%	24%
Total	29%	26%

Here the key point is that 29 per cent of those businesses with an induction and training process are satisfied, which was only 3 per cent greater than those owners who are satisfied but have no induction and training process. In our work with clients who had completed Score Your Business we found most processes were ineffective due to the induction documentation not being relevant to the actual roles being undertaken, and poor implementation of the process where team members were still not 100 per cent clear on role expectations and how performance is measured.

Your takeaways

1. Define your values – what are your 5 to 10 everyday non-negotiable behaviours?

2. Define your purpose – what is your customer promise that you can guarantee?

3. Create your 'way we do it here' symbol (the rules of your game) – engage and empower all team members to be a leader for the 'way we do it here'.

PART III

Stage 2: Control

A pilot flying a plane can only be in control when viewing all the dashboard instruments – providing information such as altitude, speed, direction, fuel and so on. To correctly interpret the information, the pilot must follow a detailed process of checks and balances that will determine what decision to make to ensure the safety of all on board. With no information and no process to follow, decision-making can only be based on a guess.

Sporting teams compete in a competition that is defined by a season. Prior to the season commencing, the team will plan their goals – whether that be, for example, to end as premiers, in the top 4 or top 8, or simply miss relegation. From the opening game to the last game, every score is recorded and every statistic is analysed. Reviewing the performance every game and every training session allows the team to make the right decisions to keep the team on track to achieve the season's goals. A process of continual review and refinement delivers the required control over performance outcomes.

Business owners also operate in a season – called the 12-month financial year. Most business owners have no goal prior to starting their season and undertake no review of performance during the season, due to a lack of process in reporting accurate operating information. They have no scoreboard and so no control. Decisions are based on short-term outcomes because they lack longer term goals. Too many business owners only check their scoreboard after the season has finished, at which point it is too late to change the outcome.

When you think that the business owner's family security is riding on the success of the business, you would expect having control of performance to be of paramount importance. Unfortunately, this is not the case most of the time. In this part, I outline how to gain control through empowering leadership, pricing for profit, generating business intelligence to predict success, and implementing processes that deliver your promise for every ideal customer.

CHAPTER 12

Leadership begins from within

THE RABBITOHS PREMIERSHIP STORY

The South Sydney Rabbitohs are my National Rugby League (NRL) team. Growing up in Maroubra in Sydney's eastern suburbs, I lived and breathed the Rabbitohs. My late father, Perce, played lower grades and my older brother, Grant, played first grade for the Rabbitohs. I remember spending plenty of Sunday afternoons with my family on the hill at Redfern Oval watching the footy. By late afternoon nearing the end of the game, Redfern Oval would be a dust bowl, making it difficult to make out who was who as we glared into the setting sun above the old grandstand.

Afterwards, I would come home and play out the game I just watched in my front yard. I would run, jump, kick, score, tackle, pass, dummy and side step – all the while, of course, commentating the game. My neighbours must have found it very funny watching me play my imaginary game. Even though the Rabbitohs didn't win much in the late 1970s, they were great times. Cheering on the Rabbitohs are some of my fondest memories.

Fast-track to January 2014, and I am sitting at Redfern Oval with the Rabbitohs head coach, Michael 'Madge' Maguire, and we're talking about what it will take to win the NRL premiership. In the preceding two years, the Rabbitohs had been knocked out in the preliminary final, one game before the grand final. In the 2013 preliminary final, they gained an early lead over the Manly Sea Eagles of 14–nil, only to then get overrun and miss out on the grand final. Madge wanted to discuss my 'Elite Performance Framework' methodology – designed to create 'inside-out' leadership – and how I could assist him in bringing a premiership back home to Redfern.

There was a feeling at the time that the Rabbitohs didn't know how to win – that, when the opportunity presented, they didn't know what to do. The feeling was also that when under pressure, individuals didn't know their role and, worse, individuals lacked confidence in each other. They would choke. The weight of years of disappointment was carried by the current team. The last premiership, and the last grand final appearance, was back in 1971. The club had gone through 43 years of becoming conditioned to losing – 43 years of not knowing how to win, of not expecting to win, and of being used to saying, 'There's always next year'.

There is no tomorrow

Madge was very clear with me at the start of 2014. For him, there was no next year; there was no tomorrow. His vision was, 'We win the premiership in 2014. It starts today.' He knew he had the team to win it, and they had to take the opportunity that awaited. No stone would be left unturned.

For the premiership to be realised, Madge knew he had to change his leadership style. He knew he had to stand back and let the players and coaching staff take responsibility. More importantly, he knew that everyone in the organisation had to be focused on improving individual performance every day, every session, every moment.

Everyone had to believe in each other, believe in the team, and believe in the process. No matter what the score, no matter how bleak the circumstances may seem, the focus must be on the current play. Outside distractions – weather, fans, referees – didn't matter. It was all about controlling the controllable, going out there and doing your job consistently well. It was all about belief.

INSIDE-OUT LEADERSHIP

This belief Madge was reinforcing at the Rabbitohs was underpinned by the Elite Performance Framework clarifying the club's core values, which then identifies the required performance standards and behaviours. Once the framework has been defined, every individual in the organisation must buy into the 'way we do it here' (as covered in chapter 11). Every individual must own it. Every individual must lead. The 'way we do it here' must be led and driven from the inside out.

This means even the youngest and less experienced in the team are empowered to lead, and are empowered to talk to senior team members regarding their behaviour if the senior team members' behaviour is falling outside the standards. This is what inside-out leadership means. The desired culture, behaviours and standards are driven by the group. Everyone must be accountable, and it is everyone's responsibility to lead. The expectation is that everybody does the '1 percenters' when nobody was watching. You don't have to be told, it just gets done because the individual doesn't want to let the team down.

Continual reinforcement

I assisted Madge to develop the framework, and he then had the senior leaders – Greg Inglis, Sam Burgess, John Sutton and Isaac Luke – define and agree to the required behaviours and performance standards. Once it was signed off, the 'way we do it here' needed to be embedded into the DNA of the team.

Throughout the 2014 season, we developed a week-to-week communication plan that was delivered to the team. Depending on what challenges lay ahead, Madge tailored the message to ensure the team stayed focused in the moment. Madge continually looked at ways to reinforce and, importantly, stimulate the message. Different methods were used to connect and inspire the team during meetings and presentations, and even away from the club, with individual players being sent inspirational videos and messages via text. Madge ensured that every individual was 100 per cent focused.

The Rabbitohs rolled through the semifinals to advance to their first grand final since 1971. The morning of the grand final I wished Madge good luck. I received a matter of fact response: 'We are ready to win and we are going to take it'. Take it they did, defeating the Canterbury Bulldogs convincingly to win the 2014 NRL Premiership. Mt Everest was conquered. It was a proud moment to be in the dressing room after the game holding the NRL premiership trophy with my brother Grant and my eldest son Ethan. The great memories continue.

IS YOUR TEAM LEADING FROM WITHIN?

Completing the preceding part in this book – Stage 1 of the Blueprint for Success – provides you as the business owner with clarity. You now have a clear vision for what the business will become, a clear understanding of the desired financial return on investment and, importantly, a clear 'way we do it here'. Now the key: engaging and empowering the team to drive it from within.

Just like Madge instilled a razor-sharp focus in his team on the way to winning the 2014 NRL Premiership, you must do the same with your team. To achieve anything great – to really accomplish things that blow people's minds, and really set new industry standards – this process must be driven from within. You won't succeed if you need a carrot and a stick. Change will not happen if you must drive it every day.

To be a leader, you must understand that true leadership doesn't come with a title – or age, years of employment or years of experience. Leadership comes down to the choices the individual makes relating to their personal behaviour. And these choices come down to the individual being empowered with the responsibility to drive the 'way we do it here'. They must own it.

To truly empower your team, you must educate them on why it is important – every day. Yes, every day. If you are serious about this, you must invest time and effort to reinforce the 'way we do it here' every day. You need to get creative with how you communicate the message. You need to share good and bad stories to convey your message, noting that stories are the best way for individuals to learn.

Developing leadership from within takes time, a great deal of trust and mutual respect. It requires a lot of effort from all parties, but the outcomes are worth it. Leading from within is the critical first element to successfully implementing this second stage (Control) of the Blueprint for Success.

Your takeaways

1. There is no tomorrow – winning starts today.

2. Empower your team to own the 'way we do it here' – every team member is a leader.

3. Get creative with your story telling – engage and inspire your team.

CHAPTER 13

Watch out for 'growing broke'

DEATH BY A THOUSAND CUTS

What is growing broke? This is where sales are up, everyone is busy, but profit is declining and you have no money in the bank. Uncontrolled sales growth will commonly cause cash flow headaches.

While assisting business owners gain control of their business, I'm often asked, 'How come the busier I get, the less money I have in the bank?' From my personal experience, backed up by research published here and internationally, the main cause of cash flow problems is the business owner failing to manage growth.

This is a classic failing of an owner operating in the tradie mindset syndrome. This mindset dictates 'go out and sell hard'. Win big, sell lots. As a result, sales are up, the team is busy, so everything must be good, right? Wrong.

In this scenario, the owner totally failed in their number one duty: to safely position the business into the future. Because their focus was on the short term – simply winning lots of work – no consideration is given to the cost required to deliver the extra work. No consideration is given to new processes and the systems required to effectively manage the extra administration.

As work increases (but before invoices are paid), the business needs to be able to cover the cost of extra wages for new team members. But these are not the only costs that drain the business's two key resources, cash and time, as more jobs are taken on. These extra costs include those associated with:

- hiring more employees – such as recruitment and training costs, tool box talks and performance management
- expanding capacity to deliver the extra work – adding vehicles, tools and equipment, phones, insurance, warehouse space and other equipment
- increased administration – implementing job management systems, quoting, invoicing, collections, payables, payroll liability, superannuation liability and tax liability
- an increase in customer service – including quality control, compliance, defects, follow-up and meetings
- increases in material purchases – implementing the purchase order system, delivery management, inventory management, wastage and theft.

The costs associated with financing all the preceding areas can quickly drain the business's cash supply. The critical point here is that, as the company grows its sales, cash collection lags behind the cash outgoings. The result: a cash crisis and time management crisis for the business owner.

THE DANGER OF PRICING LOW TO WIN WORK

Pricing low to win work is a sure-fire way to drain the business's resources in time, capacity and cash. This strategy guarantees the business will continually struggle to pay the owner a regular wage, let alone provide the owner with any financial return on investment. As discussed in chapter 10, common pricing failures relate to not accounting for the actual financial investment required to operate the business.

Often the business owner doesn't realise they are losing money before they even get onsite. Pricing is often based on competitor rates or customer demands, with no thought given to the actual financial and time investment required to deliver the job. Basing your pricing on competitor rates doesn't make sense, especially if they are using outdated methods and old equipment and you are investing in the latest technologies that deliver a superior product and service in half the time.

To ensure you do not grow broke, accurate pricing for profit, whether hourly rate or fixed price, is required to guarantee successful growth. This starts with calculating your break-even hourly rate. To accurately calculate this point, and so price for profit, measurement of the following determining factors is required:

- your annual billable time – that is, actual chargeable or productive hours
- lost productivity time – including time lost to annual leave, travel, tool box talks, training, unproductive hours and factoring in weather
- your annual financial investment (as discussed in chapter 10)
- employee investment – including wages, workers compensation, superannuation, long service leave and leave loading
- office and administration investment – including insurances, interest, accountant and bank fees, licences, memberships, phones, internet, operating systems and rent

- equipment and vehicle investment – including leases, fuel, tolls, tools (hand/power tools), consumables and repairs
- the required profit on top of the break-even hourly rate – the profit the business must generate per chargeable hour to make it worthwhile.

Here is the story of one of our clients, let's call him Max, who operates a general maintenance business. When Max first contacted me he was struggling big time. His business had tripled in two years and he had more new clients banging down his door. As soon as cash hit the bank, however, it was gone again. He was constantly trying to keep up, the classic hamster on the wheel spinning faster and faster and yet going nowhere.

I asked Max what strategy he used to grow his business. His answer: 'price'. His current hourly rate was $70 and material margin was 10 per cent. I told Max these needed to increase, but Max said he couldn't increase the price because he would lose work. I said that was the plan and he gave me a baffled look.

After spending time estimating his annual actual chargeable hours and annual planned financial investment, I calculated his base rate or break-even hourly rate at $74 (see the following table for these workings). This was $4 above his current hourly rate of $70 per hour – which meant he was currently losing $4 per hour. Now considering Max also had a low cost of sale expense with a minimum margin of 10 per cent, offering limited contribution to the operating profit, his business was redlining – and needed help fast.

Break-even hourly rate – determining factors

Actual chargeable or productive hours	5,728
Planned financial investment	$422,431
Base rate per hour – break-even hourly rate	$74

Current hourly rates

Maintenance work hourly rate	$70

A day after refusing to increase his hourly rate, I presented the figures outlined in the preceding table. Within the blink of an eye, Max said he didn't realise he was working for nothing – and that he'd better increase his prices. He increased his hourly rate to $85 per hour and increased material margin to 30 per cent. As a result, he lost cheap clients – which left Max with more time to attract better clients, meaning profit increased, he had money in the bank and fewer headaches.

Knowing this sort of information means saying no to unprofitable jobs becomes a quick and easy process, saving you time and money.

SMARTER VERSUS HARDER STORY

During my workshops where I educate business owners on getting to know their financial numbers, I use the 'Smarter versus Harder' story to explain the concept of 'growing broke' and so help them to understand the true financial story of their business.

In this real-life story, we have two young plumbing clients, one I call 'Smarter' and the other 'Harder'. Both had been operating for three years and focusing on renovation work, and both were turning over roughly $200,000. Both businesses were delivering $60,000 in operating profit at 30 per cent, before owner drawings. When planning for the upcoming new season (the 12-month financial year) both owners predicted turnover doubling to $400,000, delivering $120,000 operating profit at 30 per cent, before owner drawings.

Fast-track to the end of the season to review their results and both achieved their turnover goal of $400,000. However, their operating profit result was a very different story. Smarter doubled his operating profit to the predicted $120,000, while Harder halved his operating profit from the previous season to $30,000. Harder went about things totally differently from Smarter. Harder ignored the Blueprint for Success methodology and was quickly inflicted again with the tradie mindset syndrome. Smarter, on the other hand, stayed focused in the business performance mindset.

The following table summarises how they operated their respective businesses that resulted in doubling turnover and delivering mixed operating profit results.

Harder – tradie mindset syndrome	Smarter – business performance mindset
• Very busy all the time – got excited with lots of work coming in • Took on jobs should have said no to • No time to plan or monitor the business – did not review financial performance scorecard during the season • Completed quotes last minute – always rushed • Incorrectly scoped and priced quotes • No material purchase order system, meaning materials not allocated to jobs • No job planning system – planning started when team arrived to site	• Took his time – not rushed • Confidently said no to a lot of jobs – did fewer jobs than Harder • Made time to plan and monitor the business – reviewed financial performance scorecard every month • Made plenty of time to finish quotes prior to due date, and triple-checked all quotes • Correctly scoped and priced all quotes • Did not waste time quoting on poor jobs • Detailed material purchase order process for each job – all materials assigned to job or inventory • Detailed job planning system – all jobs marked out, materials ordered and required equipment ordered prior to team arriving to site

The scorecard of these two approaches is shown in the following table.

The moral of the story is that increasing turnover doesn't guarantee increasing profit. Harder never worked so hard in his life, yet for all his efforts he actually halved his personal drawings from the previous year. Beware the process of 'growing broke'. You must remove all emotion and operate in the business performance mindset. If you plan to increase turnover without planning to invest more time 'on' the business through managing systems and measuring performance, then you're planning to 'grow broke'.

	Harder – growing broke			Smarter – growing profitably		
Turnover	$400,000		100% growth on prior year	$400,000		100% growth on prior year
Cost of materials	$160,000	40%	Cost increased 10% on prior year	$120,000	30%	Maintained prior year %
Gross profit	$240,000	60%	Gross profit % dropped	$280,000	70%	Gross profit % maintained
Labour (not including owner)	$120,000	30%	Increased 10% on prior year	$80,000	20%	Maintained prior year %
Expenses	$90,000	22.5%	Increased 2.5% on prior year	$80,000	20%	Maintained prior year %
Total overheads	**$210,000**	**52.5%**		**$160,000**	**40%**	
Operating profit	**$30,000**	**7.5%**	**Decreased 22.5% from prior year – profit reduced by $30,000**	**$120,000**	**30%**	**Maintained prior year % – profit increased by $60,000**

Score Your Business: Is bigger better?

The 'Score Your Business' assessment also looked at the satisfaction levels of trade service and construction business owners relating to levels of turnover and numbers of team members.

Level of satisfaction based on turnover

The assessment asked owners, 'Are you satisfied that you are achieving your personal goals? (Such as lifestyle, income, debt levels, working hours and stress level)'. The results are shown in the following table.

Turnover	Total businesses		Owners satisfied
Less than $300K	245	53%	29%
$300K–$600K	112	24%	24%
$600K–$1M	59	13%	19%
More than $1M	50	11%	24%
Total	466	100%	26%

Level of satisfaction based on number of team members

The following table breaks down level of satisfaction based on size of team.

Number of team members	Total businesses		Owners satisfied
0	172	37%	30%
1 to 3	205	44%	22%
4 to 8	65	14%	32%
More than 8	24	5%	13%
Total	466	100%	26%

The key points here are:

- Increasing turnover and increasing size of team don't automatically correlate to increased satisfaction. Only 24 per cent of business owners with turnover more than $1,000,000 are satisfied. Only 13 per cent of business owners with more than eight team members are satisfied. The research showed that owners operating at this level are enslaved to the job, putting out fires daily. Given their huge risk, and the time and money they have invested just to keep the business ticking over, the financial and personal rewards are not enough.

- Beware thinking that by simply growing your business your personal wealth and lifestyle rewards will be satisfied. Statistics show this is not the case. Successfully growing a business and increasing personal rewards are directly correlated to the level of investment in planning, preparation and execution. The greater the level of planning and preparation, and the greater the execution, the greater the level of satisfaction.

Your takeaways

1. Calculate your break-even hourly rate – and quickly say no to jobs that will cost you money.

2. Plan to grow profitably – with no plan you will grow broke.

3. Invest time to monitor performance – review systems and measure results.

CHAPTER 14

Controlling your cash flow

CAN YOU SEE THE RED TRAIN?

The majority of construction and trade service businesses are operating under pressure from inadequate cash flow. Figures released by ASIC from 2013–2014 financials reveal 24 per cent of businesses that became insolvent over this period were from the construction sector, the highest of any industry. And according to ASIC, 41 per cent of company failure was due to inadequate cash flow.

The problem for a lot of tradie business owners right now is that they have no control over their cash flow. Most do not know if the money currently sitting in their business bank account is actually theirs, or if it really belongs to their suppliers or the taxman. Day to day, week to week, month to month, large chunks of money are deposited into the bank account, and large chunks of money are debited from the bank account. For the business owner, the result is either feast or famine – money one day, none the next.

Planning must be a priority

History shows plenty of profitable businesses have failed due to a lack of cash flow. And this lack of cash flow often comes down to inadequate cash flow planning – basically, simply withdrawing more from the bank than will be deposited. This in turn is often a result of underestimating the cost to deliver the work, underestimating the cost of operating the business, overestimating the amount of income to be generated, and underestimating the time it will take for the income to hit the bank.

I always ask my business training attendees if they are using a cash flow forecaster to manage the cash going in and out of their bank account. The response is often a blank stare. Unfortunately, most small businesses fail to implement any form of cash flow forecasting and planning.

Failing to track when money will hit the bank account or when money will leave the bank account places you as the business owner in the dark, not being able to see if current cash levels are sufficient to meet future demands. For a business owner, the unknown is stressful and often fatal.

You must see the red train approaching

When business owners are operating in the dark when it comes to cash flow, they don't see the 'red train' about to run straight over the top of them. Once this red train hits, their cash is cleaned out of the bank along the way. The unsuspecting owner gets up, looks in the bank account, and only then notices it is empty – in the red. Bills and wages cannot be paid. At this point they state, 'I didn't see that coming'. If you can see the cash flow red train approaching, you can do something about it; when it has hit you, it is too late.

Business owners operating in the tradie mindset syndrome never see the red train coming. The following errors compound the problems covered in the preceding chapter relating to growing broke and incorrect pricing:

- incorrect decision making – owners spending money when they should be saving money

- inadequate terms of trade – owners failing to identity the negative cash impacts incurred through delayed invoicing and extended collection terms

- inadequate planning – failing to plan for large statutory liabilities such as GST, payroll, tax and superannuation

- inadequate sales activity – failing to identify shortfalls in the future sales pipeline (required to cover future planned expenses).

Successfully growing your business requires detailed cash flow planning that you monitor at least on a weekly basis. The recommended method is to use a 13-week rolling cash flow forecaster to enter all your planned incoming and outgoing cash. The key is to enter all your planned cash transactions even if you haven't invoiced or received the bill. Your cash flow forecaster must contain all current invoices and bills, as well as future planned invoices and bills that will occur over the 13 weeks.

Rolling 13-week cash flow forecasting provides the necessary cash flow transparency identifying any fast-approaching red trains early. This is critical to the survival and growth of all construction and trade service industry businesses – including yours.

DO YOU KNOW YOUR CASH FLOW PROFILE?

While operating my plumbing business in the 1990s I was totally unaware of cash flow planning and forecasting. All I knew was that I had a lot of jobs on at the same time. This resulted in a lot of money moving in and out of my bank account. Money in, money out. My problem was that I didn't know what was my money to stay, and what was actually going to suppliers, wages or the taxman. I was operating in the dark.

This experience led me to create a cash flow profile for each job. By splitting a job down the middle, you can see when money is coming in and going out of the bank. This visual representation is very useful for avoiding the red train.

A story of cash flow pain

The example shown in the following table is based on a trade services business with a turnover of $550,000. Australian Taxation Office statistics, based on the industry and turnover levels, tell us that, on average, this business will need to wait between 40 to 55 days to get paid once the invoice has been submitted.

The table outlines the costs going out from the business while it waits to receive payment.

When a tradie business owner is confronted with this picture, typically the first comment is something like, 'I didn't realise I had become a bank, having to finance the whole job'.

This is the problem: most business owners inflicted with the tradie mindset syndrome are unaware of their cash flow profile. They are unaware how risk-exposed they are. Again, this is operating in the dark.

	Week 1	Week 2	Week 3	Week 4	Week 5	Week 6	Week 7
	1st of month	8th of month	15th of month	23rd of month	1st of month	8th of month	15th of month
Job completed	1st of month						
Critical – invoicing delayed 7 days due to lack of automated processes.							
Job invoiced – $10,000		8th of month	Clock starts ticking on days to get paid from the date the job is invoiced				
		7 days	14 days	21 days	28 days	35 days	42 days
Critical – when you know your numbers, you know the costs of generating income relating to overheads, labour and materials.							
Overheads: cost of doing business @ 20% = $2,000	$500 – pay insurance	$500 – pay phones	$500 – pay equip	$500 – pay fees	Examples of the expenses to be withdrawn from the bank		
Labour cost of doing business @ 20% = $2,000		$1,000 – pay team		$1,000 – pay team	Example of wage component to deliver job withdrawn from the bank		
Material cost of doing business @ 30% = $3,000				$3,000 – pay suppliers	Example of direct expenses to deliver job withdrawn from the bank		
Critical – business has to carry the financial risk over this 42-day period							
Customer pays							$10,000

Operating through the lens of a business performance mindset ensures all potential risks associated with a business model are identified. Once the risks have been identified the appropriate processes and systems can be implemented to mitigate all associated risk. The processes and systems relate how to:

- *Increase invoicing efficiency and speed:* When job will be invoiced, where can invoicing take place, and how the invoice will be generated (think automated systems and clear terms and conditions)

- *Increase payment efficiency and speed:* When and how payment is to be made (again, think automated systems and clear terms and conditions)

- *Access finance to protect cash flow:* When will you require extra cash, and where will you access extra cash, for example an overdraft (think financial safety net).

When you assess the appropriate processes and systems to increase the speed at which money hits your bank account, you must think with the end in mind. You need to work out what needs to be implemented to ensure consistent cash flow without you having to jump in to quickly invoice customers or call customers to chase payment because you have no cash in the bank.

Score Your Business: How many business owners manage their cash flow?

The 'Score Your Business' assessment also looked at the level of cash flow management undertaken by trade service and construction business owners.

Business owners with a cash flow management process

Research participants were asked, 'Do you regularly forecast your cash flow position? (What will be coming into and out of your bank account each week)'. Their responses are shown in the following table.

Turnover	With a cash flow management process	As % of total
Less than $300K	73	30%
$300K–$600K	44	39%
$600K–$1M	22	37%
More than $1M	27	54%
Total	**166**	**36%**

The key points here are:

- A lack of cash flow contributes to business failure. This is due to the fact that, based on the research, overall only 36 per cent of business owners forecast their cash flow on a weekly basis. Most business owners are operating blind relating to their cash flow requirements.

- For businesses with a turnover of more than $1,000,000, 54 per cent have a weekly cash flow management process in place.

Level of satisfaction based on having a cash flow management process

Satisfaction levels for businesses with and without a cash flow management process in place, broken down by turnover, are shown in the following table.

Turnover	With a cash flow management process and satisfied achieving personal goals	No cash flow management process and satisfied achieving personal goals
Less than $300K	47%	22%
$300K–$600K	34%	18%
$600K–$1M	23%	16%
More than $1M	30%	17%
Total	37%	20%

The key point here is that implementing a cash flow management process increases business owner satisfaction levels. Increased control of cash flow provides peace of mind for the business owner. As turnover increases, satisfaction declines for those business owners with no cash flow management process.

Your takeaways

1. Implement weekly cash flow planning – set up a 13-week rolling cash flow forecaster to gain control of your cash.

2. Increase the speed of your invoicing – implement appropriate systems and terms for your type of work to consistently invoice on time.

3. Increase speed of payment – again, implement appropriate systems and terms for your type of work to consistently get paid on time.

CHAPTER 15

Business intelligence predicts success

LOOK AT THE CAUSE NOT THE SYMPTOMS

Business owners who are not satisfied with their current performance often talk about their perceived problems: no money, no time, no holidays, no direction, poor clients, tired all the time. However, these are not the problems. These are the symptoms. To fully operate in the business performance mindset, you must focus on the cause, not the symptoms. The cause of all symptoms can be traced back to prior decision making. Any symptom you're currently experiencing directly relates back to decisions you made one day ago, one week ago, one month ago or even one year ago. As author and speaker Jim Rohn notes, 'Failure is not a single, cataclysmic event. You don't fail overnight. Instead, failure is a few errors in judgment, repeated every day.'

The following table outlines common symptoms (often described by business owners as problems) and their likely causes and outcomes.

Symptom (*not* problem)	Cause	Outcome
No money at the end of the job	Poor quoting system	Did not account for required materials and labour and so under-charged for job
No money at the end of the job	Poor material management	Material not tracked leading to high wastage and job not billed correctly
No money at the end of the job	Poor variation management	Variations not tracked or signed off meaning materials and labour invested but not charged
No time – constantly spinning on the hamster wheel	Not knowing which customers to say no to	Saying yes to jobs for poor clients that cost time
No time – constantly spinning on the hamster wheel	Poor internal processes	Owner always jumping in to get things done – wearing all the hats in the business
No good tradespeople	Hiring too fast – no team selection or training process	Individuals employed who were not suited – did not believe in the 'way we do it here'

The real cause behind most problems faced by business owners is poor decision-making when stuck in the tradie mindset syndrome. Due to the nature of this mindset, decisions are made with a lack of complete and relevant information delivered real time. Generally, very limited research is conducted. This means decisions are based on 'gut feel' or raw emotion. This does result in some wins, but also comes with a lot of losses, leading to a cycle of 'boom and bust'.

Be aware of the symptoms

Operating a business today is tough. Often business owners succumb to their operating landscape by failing to safely navigate the 4 Cs (competition, customer, compliance and cloud) and the issues associated with these. (For more on the 4 Cs, refer to chapter 7.)

One wrong decision in this landscape can create often fatal symptoms and so can spell the end for any business, no matter how previously successful they were. In chapter 7, I cover the problems that can arise through failing to safely navigate the 4 Cs. As a business owner now operating in the business performance mindset, you must be aware of these problems and start to see them more as symptoms. These symptoms and possible causes include the following:

1   *Investing lots and lots of time and money managing multiple operating systems:* These operating systems relate to accounting, job management, quoting, and sales and marketing. This is particularly a problem if you still have no confidence in the accuracy of the data and information produced.

   Common causes: The initial decision to purchase the system was based on doing the specific task quicker and easier, today. No thought was given to how these systems would contribute to longer term business decisions. Because focus was short term, the system is set up incorrectly for the specific needs of the business, and a lack of adequate training was invested in learning how to operate the system. Simply put: rubbish in equals rubbish out.

2   *Lots and lots and lots of meaningless data:* Poor information leads to emotional decision-making. Decisions become kneejerk reactions to what is best for today, rather than what is in the best interests of the business in the longer term. This short-term view is based on what needs to be done now, no long-term view is considered. When it comes down to selecting where to invest time and choosing between 'important actions' and 'urgent tasks', urgent tasks always win.

Common causes: The multiple operating systems often run independently, with the data housed in separate silos. In the initial set-up stage, no thought was given to how the data needs to be reported and analysed. This results in data becoming meaningless and redundant. Data only becomes valuable information when it is sliced and diced against all operating data, which is then measured against performance predictors to assist decision-making. This is the beginning of true business intelligence.

3   *Business is moving way too fast:* This is a feeling of 'no hands on the wheel' and no clarity regarding what to look out for. The owner has no understanding of what are the right things to do at the right time.

Common causes: The general lack of integrated system data means the owner is unable to get a clear picture of all sides of the business at once. Because things are moving fast, for example, you see that sales are down, so you pull the trigger to ramp up sales. This decision is made without looking at all sides of the business, such as how ramping up sales will affect cash flow, resource capacity or customer experience. When the business is moving very fast, the business owner is always looking for the most direct route to get from A to B, in the shortest possible time. As mentioned in chapter 7, this is like setting sail with only a compass in hand – but without analysing the tide charts, the weather forecast, or what craft will suit the prevailing conditions. This means you face a good chance of sailing straight into a storm.

BREAK THE OLD MOULD

For business owners operating with no awareness of the potential fatal symptoms, my prediction is continued pain. To avoid this pain, you need to break old hard-wiring to understand business doesn't have to be this hard. You must break the old mould of thinking that running a business is hard – because it doesn't have to be.

Operating in a business performance mindset allows you to search for new ways to break old-school conditioning. You need to break the old way of thinking. Remove frustration, and replace it with clarity and control. Aim to move away from working a job that controls you, towards operating a business that serves you.

Rather than get a lot of things done, stop the hamster wheel and get the one right thing done. Move from thinking everything is important, and not being able to prioritise or manage time, to having razor-sharp focus in getting the important things done.

Move away from being inundated with a lot of meaningless data, and towards information that provides business intelligence. Understand how the business is performing and, with certainty, know what triggers need to be pulled to increase productivity, efficiency and profit. You need to gain 100 per cent control of your business and its financials.

Throw away the unsustainable business model that is sucking your money, time and life. Create a business model that delivers consistent money, and frees up your time to provide a life of choice. Forget liquidation and bankruptcy; think abundance and prosperity. Forget no quality family time; think lifestyle of choice filled with great family and lifestyle memories.

WHERE HAS MY PROFIT GONE?

Where has my profit gone? This is one of the most common questions I get asked from business owners who have financial statements reporting the business has generated an operating profit, but they have no cash in the bank. The business owner immediately thinks the financial statements are incorrect – how can the business be profitable yet have no cash? *This doesn't make sense,* they think. *This cannot be right, I don't trust the numbers.*

The real cause of many a business failure begins with a general lack of financial understanding. The thought process is something along the lines of, *Why should I try to understand the numbers relating to my financial performance when they are incorrect in the first place?* The question the owner wants answered is, 'What does the financial information mean and what do I need to do today to guarantee more cash in the bank?'

From my experience, the reason most business owners lack financial understanding is because they rely on accounting systems that are set up for the sole purpose of reporting tax liability. These accounting systems are implemented with the sole aim of reporting the past. The focus is looking back not looking forward. This often results in owners receiving financial information that isn't relatable or easily interpreted, and isn't timely. In other words, this information doesn't help the owner make better decisions today. 'I am busy with a lot of people waiting for me to make a decision,' these owners say. 'Please just tell me what I need to do.'

For most business owners, historical financial reporting is confusing. They receive multiple statements reporting profit and loss, and the balance sheet listing assets and liabilities, but these offer no real meaning. The result is viewed as 'accountants speak' that is only important at tax time when all your transactions are finally reconciled.

Getting back to the original question: 'Where has my profit gone?' Our clients who are now operating with a business performance mindset know the answer to this question. Using 'The CUBE' business intelligence reporting platform all client financial statements are integrated in real time, including profit and loss, balance sheet and cash flow. This one view provides transparency relating to the impact on cash flow due to increased personal drawings, drawn out payment terms, or investing too much in vehicles and equipment. Importantly, the language is relatable to how the business operates on a day-to-day basis, making it easy to understand where profit is going. This is the sort of real-time financial information you should be accessing in your business too, so you know exactly how your cash flow is looking every day.

BUSINESS INTELLIGENCE MAKES DECISION-MAKING SIMPLE

For most business owners, knowing what decision to make becomes a hard process. Why? Because the information and data used to make the decision is often inaccurate, lacking in detail and old. This information is what I call meaningless data because it doesn't assist the decision-making process. This means decision-making is based on 'gut feel' or emotion, which invariably ends with a poor decision being made.

Operating with a business performance mindset demands educated decision-making to ensure the business is positioned for success long term. Educated decision-making is based on having real-time business intelligence highlighting predictive outcomes. Having all the necessary information collated to provide predictive outcomes makes decision-making easy. Business intelligence also makes answering the question 'Where has my profit gone?' easy and, importantly, you do not have to rely on others to provide it for you.

From my experience, the following systems and reporting deliver the necessary business intelligence to enable educated decision-making:

- *Business development system:* A 12-month sales pipeline measures the number of leads, quotes and won jobs against the monthly sales target. This system assists decision-making relating to business development activity and capacity planning. With accurate information entered, you are notified on the months that require more sales based on your capacity in billable hours. For example, if sales are predicted to be very high for future months, you are notified well in advance that more billable hours are required, making the decision to increase the size of team an easy one.

- *Pricing system:* This system is set up to price for profit. All rates are based on calculating the break-even hourly rate, which takes into account the predicted annual billable or productive hours, annual financial investment, and the desired annual profit goal, as previously discussed in chapter 13. If a client pushes back to a lower price, you can more easily walk away because you know you are pricing to deliver a predicted profit. Pricing is not based on turnover or keeping the team busy.

- *Capacity planning system:* Required capacity in actual billable or productive hours is based on delivering the predicted sales targets. The capacity planning system needs to be integrated with the business development system. As predicted sales increase, the required billable hours increase. As predicted sales decrease, the required billable hours decrease. The important point here is that the business intelligence is predicting performance months in advance, giving you plenty of time to make great proactive decisions. No more surprises.

- *Cash flow system:* Cash flow planning is critical before making any commitment to deploy your resources. As discussed in chapter 14, you require the business intelligence to predict if a decision will commit you to a head-on collision with the red train. Business intelligence notifies you well in advance if you have the cash flow necessary to undertake predicted jobs based on your cash flow profile.

- *Your performance scoreboard:* Accurate recording and reporting of all system data measured against periodic performance targets provides a prediction of the season's result. The scoreboard highlights systems requiring attention – relating to, for example, business development, quoting, material management, labour planning and payment terms. The performance scoreboard predicts well in advance the financial return on investment for the 12-month season.

With systems delivering great business intelligence, decision-making becomes easy. You quickly get to a 'Go or No Go' point where a decision can be made. Great data in, measured against required parameters, equates to great decisions. Of course, once the decision is made, a lot of things can happen that are out of our control. The important point here is that you were in control of the initial 'Go or No Go' decision, and will remain in control on a daily basis with real-time business intelligence.

The following chapters develop these ideas further, looking at processes to implement.

Score Your Business:
How many business owners have
12-month financial targets?

The 'Score Your Business' assessment also asked the 466 trade service and construction business owners whether they had designed clear 12-month financial targets.

Business owners with 12-month financial targets

The research asked owners, 'Do you meet with your advisor or accountant *before* the start of the financial year? (Confirming 12-month financial forecasts, including profit, ensuring appropriate business structures, tax planning and investment planning)'. The following table shows the responses.

Turnover	With 12-month financial targets	As % of category
Less than $300K	89	36%
$300K–$600K	52	46%
$600K–$1M	29	49%
More than $1M	24	48%
Total	194	42%

The key points to note here are:

- Only 42 per cent of business owners set out prior to the start of the financial year with clarity relating to how they want their business to be designed. Most business owners are running blind with regards to what they want their investment in the business to deliver.

- With no external support, no direction and no financial targets in place, the owner cannot design a sustainable business. Incorrect business structure choice and no tax planning leads to increased exposure to potential risks and increased liabilities.

Level of satisfaction based on having 12-month financial targets

How satisfied are business owners with or without 12-month financial targets were is shown in the following table.

Turnover	With 12-month financial targets and satisfied achieving personal goals	No 12-month financial targets and satisfied achieving personal goals
Less than $300K	43%	22%
$300K–$600K	29%	20%
$600K–$1M	21%	17%
More than $1M	29%	19%
Total	34%	21%

The point to note here is that 34 per cent of business owners with financial targets are satisfied, compared with only 21 per cent with no financial target. The key to this satisfaction is through having the business intelligence measuring and predicting performance. This provides owners with the control to make educated decisions required to guarantee desired financial rewards.

Your takeaways

1. Assess the actual causes of your current problems – long-term solutions focus on the causes, whereas short-term fixes focus on the symptom.

2. Implement systems that deliver business intelligence – business intelligence results in proactive educated decision-making, while meaningless data results in reactive kneejerk reactions.

3. Having a scoreboard delivering business intelligence highlights required performance that will guarantee results.

CHAPTER 16

Process, process, process ... sets you free

GET OUT OF THE WAY – IT'S NOT ALL ABOUT YOU

Most business owners have a fear of letting go. They struggle to come to terms with the fact that the business, with the appropriate systems in place, can operate just fine without them. These kinds of owners feel they need to part of every decision, every transaction and every discussion. Ultimately, they are the reason the business is not flourishing.

Along with the owner not letting go, businesses fail due to the owner's general lack of focus. This lack of focus always starts and stops with a lack of confidence in their own decision-making. In turn, this lack of confidence often sees decisions being changed quickly due to the business hitting some turbulence on the journey, and panic setting in. So, where does the confidence come from? The answer is *process*. Successful business people build confidence through focusing on process.

Process enables owners to build an insanely successful business that will serve them. Yes, to be insanely successful requires only one word: process! Process allows owners to confidently delegate responsibility, and ensures consistent performance when the owner is not there. Importantly, process guarantees the owner will have freedom from the job, breaking the shackles of the day-to-day operation that have enslaved the owner.

However, most people never invest the time to develop and implement adequate process. Why? Well, the common response I receive is, 'I haven't got the time'. Here the tradie mindset syndrome is talking again. You must listen to yourself speak. You must catch yourself when you're speaking through the tradie mindset syndrome.

When a business owner tells me they haven't got time to implement process, I hear something else entirely. To illustrate this, let's look at the story of 'Tom the Tradie'. Tom rings me up. 'Hi Jonesy, I am soooooooooo busy right now. You do not understand. I cannot step aside from the job.' *I am thinking, Here we go again. Another business owner who thinks that their business is different from every other business in the world.* Business owners who think like this need to get over their own self-importance. In simple terms, for the business to be successful, you must first get out of the way to realise it is not all about you.

Tom continues, 'I have jobs piled high, I have customers chasing me, I have my team chasing me, I have quotes piled high, I have invoices piled high, I have to recruit another tradesman, I have suppliers chasing me for payment, and I have my accountant chasing me to fix up the BAS from last year. Jonesy, I hear what you are saying about process, but I cannot afford to take one hour away from the work at this stage.'

Invest time today or waste time tomorrow

Do you hear what Tom is saying? He is saying rather than invest one hour today, which would ultimately free up time tomorrow, he is happy to continue to waste time. We now live in a world where social media is driving 'instant gratification' and the 'wanting it now' mentality. The all-too-familiar comment I hear is, 'I do not have time to build credibility, systems or partnerships; I just want the end result now'. The 'result' referred to here is cash, cars and an improved lifestyle. However, any perceived success is always short-lived without process.

Let's translate tradie mindset syndrome language into the language of an owner operating in a business performance mindset. 'Hi Jonesy, I know that investing one hour a week on developing and implementing processes will remove me from having to do the task myself. This will then save me hours, days and weeks of my time – currently wasted because I continually complete the task myself, or have to micromanage others doing it. Having processes in place will save me time and mean I don't have to jump back in and do it myself. So it makes logical sense to schedule time in my calendar each week to invest in process. This is a key rock in my calendar that cannot be moved.'

It all comes down to mindset. With the right mindset, you will make the right choices. In the following section, I share with you how process can transform even the worst performing business into an insanely successful business. I am very fortunate to see this success firsthand with my clients, who transform their businesses simply through implementing the required processes. This is where the true magic is. Get this right and enjoy long-term sustainable success.

One further point to think about: how can McDonald's employ teenagers to operate multimillion-dollar businesses all over the world? By implementing a 'turnkey' operation where process dictates every decision. Every potential task has a clearly defined process. Each process has been designed to guarantee delivery of a consistent product and service. Every team member is trained how to confidently operate the process. Every team member knows that if the process is not followed, a breakdown in delivery will occur. Simple.

THE SUCCESS CYCLE – START WITH PROCESS

The success cycle is summarised in the following figure.

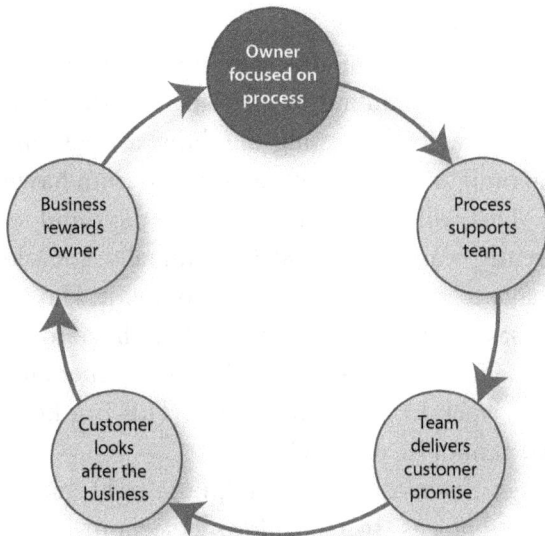

Here is the success cycle guaranteed:

1   *Owner focuses on the process:* Using business intelligence (such as sales and profit data, productivity and capacity data), the owner makes educated business decisions in terms of what process requires investment to develop. The owner identifies the right process to improve today to ensure the business meets the demands of tomorrow. A simple way to start is at the beginning. What is your process to profile leads?

How can you qualify the lead accurately to ensure you do not waste time on meetings and on quoting for 'tyre kickers'? The owner takes care of the process, knowing this is the secret to any insanely successful business.

2   *Process supports the team:* Based on the vision, purpose and 'way we do it here', all processes must be designed to deliver consistency across all areas of the business. This includes marketing, sales, recruitment, onsite, accounts and reporting. Process supports the team through providing the required information, training and structure for them to be successful in their individual roles.

3   *Team delivers the customer promise:* Process allows the team to completely focus on the customers' needs. The team is inspired to achieve the business purpose and deliver the customer promise. Everyone takes ownership and all believe in the processes. The team looks after the customer by following the process.

4   *Customer looks after the business:* The team consistently delivers on the customer promise, creating very happy customers. The customer experience is always consistent. From the initial phone call to the job being completed to the follow-up, everything the team does is customer-focused. These customers look after the business through becoming brand advocates, spreading the good word and building quality referral business.

5   *Business rewards the owner:* A business delivering consistent successful results for their customers will deliver personal wealth and lifestyle rewards for the owner. The business rewards the owner through a healthy financial return on investment. The owner is excited and prepared to further invest in the process!

When operating in the tradie mindset syndrome the owner mistakenly focuses on the customer with the hope of extracting as much value and money as possible now. Investing in systems and training the team is not a priority; the priority is all about just getting the job done. This type of focus is short term, resulting in the team being unsupported, customers being underwhelmed and a business that is underperforming and draining the owner's time, energy and potential wealth (as shown in the following figure).

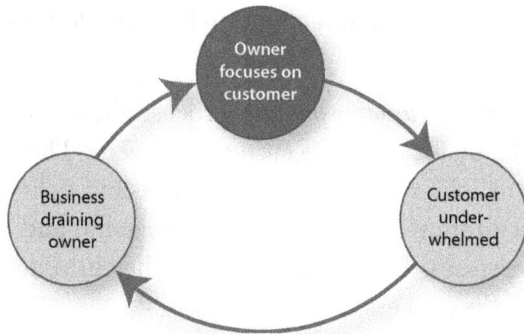

CONTINUALLY IMPROVING YOUR PROCESSES

If you are a business owner whose goal is to build a business that can be operated under management, without the day-to-day input from you as the owner, then simply focus on process. Process sets business owners free from having to work in the business 24/7.

Your priority is to operate in a business performance mindset – and adopting this mindset means you clearly understand the importance of investing in process today to reap the long-term benefits. No 'quick fix' exists when building a business that serves the owner in the long term. You must make process the priority.

To commence your focus on process, develop a mind map that identifies all the day-to-day tasks undertaken within the business. See the following figure for an example mind map that identifies the tasks associated with receiving a lead and creating a job in the system.

Once this has been completed, you need to produce a 'how-to' procedure guide that lists all the necessary steps to successfully complete the task. Next, nominate a role within the business who is responsible for the task, and then that nominated person is inducted, trained and signed off to perform the task.

Now that another person is conducting tasks that you were previously responsible for, your next focus is on researching how tasks can now be automated through technology. This now becomes an exciting time as you become free of the business.

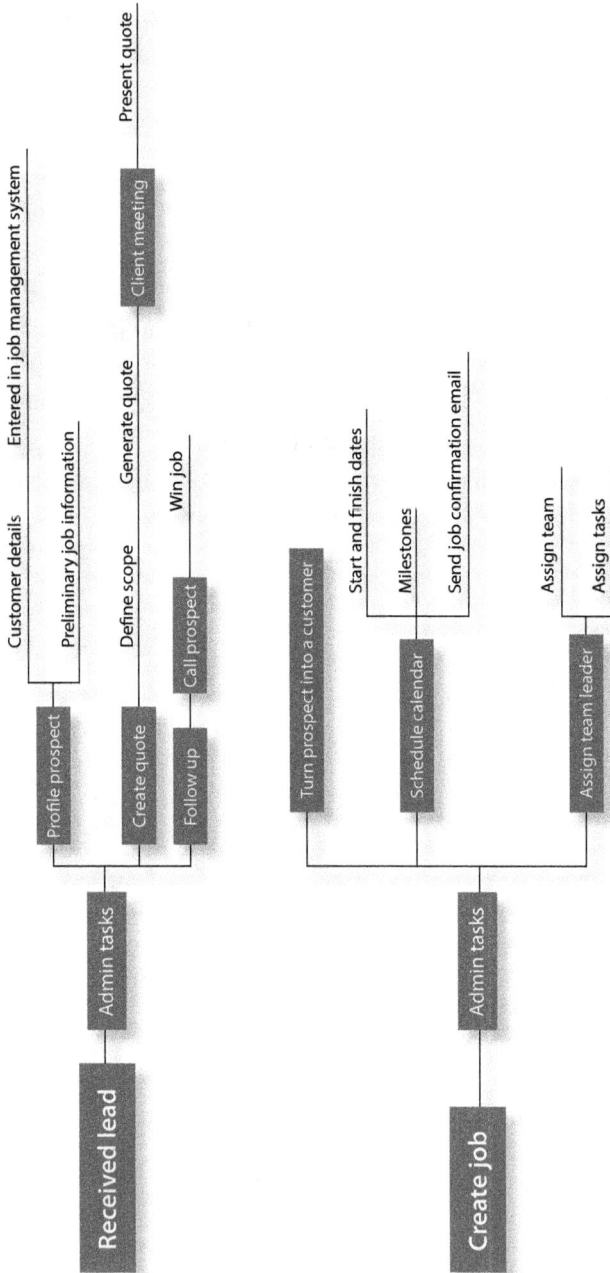

Score Your Business: How many business owners have systems?

The 'Score Your Business' assessment also asked the 466 trade service and construction business owners about their systems in place and the level of automation within the business.

Business owners using job management software

Owners were asked, 'Do you schedule and manage jobs using a software system? (Record hours and materials, invoice and take payment onsite)'. Their responses are shown in the following table.

Turnover	With a software job management system	As % of category
Less than $300K	78	32%
$300K–$600K	45	40%
$600K–$1M	28	47%
More than $1M	26	52%
Total	177	38%

The key point here is that, as turnover increases, so does the reliance on software to automate job management. As the number of tasks increases, automation becomes a priority.

The assessment then looked at business owners' levels of satisfaction based on using a software job management system. The following table shows the results in this area.

Turnover	With a software job management system and satisfied achieving personal goals	No software job management system and satisfied achieving personal goals
Less than $300K	36%	26%
$300K–$600K	31%	19%
$600K–$1M	18%	19%
More than $1M	19%	29%
Total	**29%**	**24%**

Here the point to note is that only a 5 per cent difference exists between the rates of business owners who are satisfied, either using or not using software. My research finds that a large number of business owners have invested in the wrong type of software that doesn't meet their business needs, and/or have failed to adequately implement the software throughout the business. In this case the business owner is not satisfied with the outcomes based on their investment in the time and money required to change the operations of the business.

Business owners using an automated quoting system

The assessment also asked owners, 'Do you use a pricing template system that is automated to quickly and accurately price jobs? (Based on specific work type, correct labour rates, correct material costs and margins)'. The following table outlines the responses.

Turnover	With an automated quoting system	As % of category
Less than $300K	81	33%
$300K–$600K	39	35%
$600K–$1M	31	53%
More than $1M	21	42%
Total	**172**	**37%**

The key point here is that 42 per cent of businesses with more than $1,000,000 turnover use automated quoting systems, lower than the 52 per cent with this level of turnover using software job management systems. This increased use of job management software relates to maintenance businesses, where quoting is often not required.

The research then looked at the level of owner satisfaction based on using an automated quoting system. Responses here are shown in the following table.

Turnover	With an automated quoting system and satisfied achieving personal goals	No automated quoting system and satisfied achieving personal goals
Less than $300K	38%	25%
$300K–$600K	31%	21%
$600K–$1M	26%	11%
More than $1M	33%	17%
Total	34%	22%

The point here is that satisfaction increases substantially for business owners using automated quoting systems. Automation of pricing and quoting saves time and increases the profitability of jobs, which then increases the personal rewards of the owner.

Business owners have terms and conditions signed

Business owners were asked, 'Do you have customers sign your terms and conditions agreement *prior* to commencing a job? (Stating how you want to do business relating to payment terms, milestones, and itemising inclusions and exclusions)'. The following table shows their responses.

Turnover	Have terms and conditions signed	As % of category
Less than $300K	59	24%
$300K–$600K	35	31%
$600K–$1M	29	49%
More than $1M	18	36%
Total	141	30%

Here, a low 30 per cent of overall businesses surveyed have terms and conditions signed before commencing the job. Having no signed terms and conditions places business owners in a vulnerable position in relation to payments being withheld due to the client not agreeing to what was delivered. Even if the scope is agreed verbally, it must be documented and signed.

Again the level of satisfaction was next assessed, this time based on having terms and conditions signed. The following table outlines these satisfaction levels.

Turnover	Have terms and conditions signed and satisfied achieving personal goals	No terms and conditions signed and satisfied achieving personal goals
Less than $300K	32%	28%
$300K–$600K	31%	21%
$600K–$1M	21%	17%
More than $1M	28%	22%
Total	29%	25%

The research shows the majority of processes relating to terms and conditions are inadequate in protecting the business owner. Often, they are lacking the necessary detail, or are not even relevant to the type of work being undertaken. Like all processes and systems, investment in time is required to ensure they are accurate and relevant to deliver any value to the business; otherwise, they are no use.

Your takeaways

1. To build a business that can operate effectively without you, focus on process – this is your priority.

2. Identify the key processes that will free up your time and drive efficiency – create a mind map to document all your tasks.

3. Continually review and improve all processes – ensure your processes consistently support the team to deliver a consistent customer experience.

Case study:
Telstra Trades Assist work
management software

I am very excited to being partnering with Telstra in developing the Trades Assist work management software platform. This platform is designed to help tradie business owners be successful at business. Trades Assist is not designed to simply help schedule and invoice more jobs. The vision is to provide business owners with an operating system that provides support for their team, guarantees customer satisfaction and creates a business that serves their personal goals.

Trades Assist is very exciting for tradie business owners. The software platform integrates with innovative business tools (including 'The CUBE') and applications that will change the way business owners operate their business. Trades Assist delivers proactive asset management, real-time predictive business intelligence and access to the 'Blueprint for Success' framework tools and information.

For more Trades Assist information go to www.tradesassist.com.au.

CHAPTER 17

Profiling your ideal client

BECOME MASTERS OF THE PROBLEM

Why do people buy anything? People buy things (products or services) to solve problems. The more problems you solve, the more valuable you become. As a business owner, your priority is to become the masters of your ideal client's problem. Study their problem, search for the best solution and focus on being the best at solving their problem. Your ability to make money is directly proportionate to how well you solve problems for your clients.

I recommend focusing on one specific customer type. This specific customer will have a unique set of problems that requires a unique solution. This is where focus is paramount – it's what turns you into a master. Coming up with your solution requires research into world's best practice, identifying the latest and greatest tools, material and equipment, and, importantly, investing time in conducting great conversations with your existing clients – conversations that unlock other potential problems relating to your client.

Where there is a problem, there is an opportunity. Where there is an opportunity, there is profit.

Investing time to go deep into the problem, to truly understand your customer's problem, is the key to dominating your market in the long term – over the next 5, 10 or 20 years. Diving deep will force you to find new solutions to solve the problem. This will drive innovation within your team and excite your customers, ensuring you are remembered. In the information age, if you are not remembered by your customer you are quickly forgotten by the market. When you are forgotten, you can expect pain – the pain of having to compete on price at every turn. Why? Because you lack the credibility of being the master of your customers' problems.

WHAT IS THE ACTUAL PROBLEM?

As an example of a customer's actual problem, consider what a property manager's actual problem is. Their problem is not that a tenant needs hot water, for example. The property manager's actual problem is that they have to manage 300 properties – meaning 300 owners and at least 300 tenants. They are under the pump with the daily headaches of responding to emails and phone calls, along with people dropping in to the office unannounced requesting answers. A tenant calling to find out when the tradie is turning up to fix the hot water is just the most recent issue. On top of this, the property manager needs to manage their internal business reporting requirements.

Their actual problem is finding someone they can trust to remove their headaches. Which tradie can they trust to turn up when they promise? Which tradie can they trust to fix the hot water first time and to leave the property cleaner than when they arrived? Which tradie can they trust to provide an invoice with all the required information? Which tradie can they trust to ultimately make their life easier so they can get on with their important tasks, rather than responding to things that should just get done? Which tradie can they trust to just get the job done?

Empathise with your client's pain

To gain trust you must empathise with your client's situation. You must demonstrate that you have invested the time in understanding their actual problem, and that you have the best solution to their problem. You need to show that you care about your client. In relation to the example of the property manager, you must communicate an understanding of the problems they face to show you empathise with their situation.

This is where most trade service business owners get it wrong. They do not empathise with their client's pain. They do not communicate that their solution is a remedy for the pain. Let me illustrate with an example.

Tom the Tradie needs more work, today. He is finding it tough at the moment with a lot of new competitors entering the market who are undercutting him on price. He is finding the construction market tough with builders going for the cheapest price. He also does some real estate maintenance work, so he thinks he will push this market. He is now becoming desperate, however, because he has no money in the bank.

He makes a plan to spend the day driving around to all the local real estate offices. He drops into 15 real estates unannounced. He asks at the reception desk for the property manager, who is unavailable. He leaves a card and asks for the manager to call him if they have any work. Tom leaves frustrated. Quite often, the card goes straight into the bin because the receptionist experiences this every day – tradies rocking up looking for work, basically expecting a hand out.

What is wrong here? First of all, Tom is operating in the classic tradie mindset syndrome. He waited until he had no work before he acted on business development. Business development only became a priority once his existing work had dried up. Because he was in a panic, he put in no planning and no preparation prior to visiting the real estate agents. He had no empathy relating to his target client, the property manager. He rocked up unannounced, and communicated that it was all about him when he basically stated, 'Give me a job'.

KNOW WHO YOU WANT TO PARTNER WITH

Now, let's look at Bill the Businessperson, who operates in the business performance mindset. Firstly, Bill knows that business development is part of his weekly routine. A key focus for him is always building the sales pipeline with potential new ideal clients. He doesn't take a 'scatter gun' approach, targeting all potential clients, but instead takes a very focused approach, targeting only ideal clients.

Bill understands it takes time to build a win–win relationship. It takes time to research and create a profile of target clients, and to understand their 'unique actual problem'. This might involve searching the potential client's website, scanning reviews, questioning the network to find anyone who has worked with them before and, importantly, identifying the key decision-maker who allocates the work. The key now is to find a creditable source who knows this key decision-maker – someone who can provide a warm introduction that will allow you to bypass the receptionist 'gatekeeper'.

This information is critical. With this 'client intelligence' you gain a valuable insight into the DNA of the organisation. Do they believe in long-term value or short-term cheapness? Are they professional and do they pay on time? What is their vision, what are their values, do they care about their clients and, importantly, what problems are they looking to solve? And, yes, finding answers to all these questions does take time. And, yes, it is worth the investment.

If you are 'cap in hand' needing work today, however, research is the last thing you are thinking about.

Pitch your promise

During this research stage, Bill can make a decision on whether or not the target client is worth pursuing. Bill now has a clear picture of who they are, including their problems and whether Bill's business has the best solution to solve these problems. This is what separates the great performing businesses from the mediocre performing businesses. Rather than the tradie mindset syndrome short-term focus, where it is all about the job, Bill's business performance mindset long-term focus is about business relationships. Bill understands the potential damage caused to his brand, his cash flow and, importantly, his time if he chooses the wrong type of client.

If the decision is to proceed, Bill must now 'pitch his promise' to the key decision-maker. Bill must clearly articulate his understanding of their problem, their values and their expectations. Bill must state how he will solve their problem, and paint the picture of what benefits will be received.

With a warm introduction made to the key decision-maker, Bill makes the call to introduce himself and his business. The conversation relates to what their problems are. Bill asks insightful questions to ensure he gains insightful answers. Prior to hanging up, Bill scheduled a time to meet where he could pitch his promise.

Based on all the information gathered during the research phase and from the discussion with the decision-maker, Bill creates a personalised pitch. The structure of the pitch begins with Bill expressing his understanding of the client's vision, values and problem. It is all about them, not Bill. At this stage, the potential client is likely impressed that Bill knows so much about them – indeed, they're likely in shock that a tradie actually empathises with their situation.

Next, Bill presents his promise, guaranteed. He then walks through his solution, detailing the investment in team, systems, processes and equipment that will guarantee delivery of his promise. Now Bill presents current customers just like the prospect, where he has delivered the solution and delivered on his promise, using testimonials and case studies to provide the required credibility.

Importantly, at the end of the meeting Bill presents the prospect with a personalised, professionally bound, 'expression of interest' document detailing the pitch. This document clearly communicates the message of what is in it for them. Bill wants to ensure the key decision-maker can share his information internally.

All these efforts make it so compelling to do business with Bill that it becomes a no-brainer. Note you may not win work immediately, but you will not be forgotten when the next opportunity presents.

Your takeaways

1. Identify your profiled customers' actual problems – and implement solutions to solve the problems.

2. Always pitch your promise – invest time in creating your 'expression of interest' document that empathises with your customer to build your credibility.

3. Practise, practise, practise delivering your pitch – train your team to be experts at articulating the pitch.

Case study:
Never giving up on a relationship

My client, let's call them A1 Plumbing, provides plumbing maintenance services to residential real estate property managers. They had lost several real estate clients due to problems with their service delivery. They were unable to keep up with the workload and they were starting to drop the ball by not delivering on their promise.

I reviewed A1 Plumbing processes with owners Sam & Jo to identify the cause of the delivery breakdowns. Once we identified that work orders must be allocated within an hour, an appropriate process was implemented. We then tested the new process before reintroducing A1 Plumbing to their real estate clients who had been disappointed with the service.

A meeting was scheduled with all the property managers for each real estate. Firstly, and most importantly, Sam opened the meeting with accepting 100 per cent responsibility for all the previous incidents where issues arose. There was no blame from Sam, only accountability. Sam then articulated how he empathised with the property managers' situation in relation to how much pressure they were under to perform their role.

By this stage, the property managers' guards had come down because they appreciated that Sam had taken responsibility for past issues and was showing interest in what was important to them. Next, Sam pitched his promise. He backed this promise up with a walk through of the newly implemented work order allocation process. This process was designed to guarantee delivery of his promise.

The outcome of this meeting was that A1 Plumbing was not only reinstated as a supplier, but also granted preferred status, leading to increased work orders for better quality and more profitable jobs. This case study highlights that you should never give up on a good relationship and you should continually improve processes to eliminate your clients' problems.

PART IV

Stage 3: Confidence

Confidence is key to success, be it personal, sport or business. And confidence is generated through having achieved previous success, having been there and done that. Experience provides the knowledge on how to plan for desired results and the ability to control performance to deliver the desired results.

When making decisions, as the business owner you must be confident you are making the right call – confident to say no to a job, to increase price and to hire more team members. This confidence is built from having business intelligence information that can predict the future results based on today's decision.

When a team has belief in the 'way we do it here' to deliver value as promised to the customer, confidence builds. As confidence increases throughout the team, positive momentum builds in attracting the right type of customers and the right type of team members. Momentum allows you as the owner to confidently predict future results based on maintaining today's performance levels. Put simply, you have confidence that the decisions being made will position the business for success well into the future.

CHAPTER 18

Price for profit *not* to be busy

In chapter 10 I discuss the importance of thinking about profit rather than just turnover. Tradies often think 'profit' is a dirty word. We don't want to talk about profit. We just think turnover. As a business owner, however, you must think profit first. As I've already mentioned, profit is your financial return on your investment in time and money, and your reward for taking on huge risk operating your business.

Without profit, you have no funds to reinvest in the business. Without profit, you cannot invest to innovate new improved ways to solve your customers' problems. Without profit you cannot invest in the training and development of your team, and you cannot contribute to the local community. Without profit, the business is on constant life support through a lack of cash.

How can you confidently guarantee profit? By pricing for profit. The mistake owners operating in the tradie mindset syndrome make is they calculate pricing that only covers costs, without including profit. Another common error is setting prices based on competitors, with no calculation at all. The problem here is even though you may be investing in superior equipment, delivering a far superior solution for your customer, you are basing your value against competitors.

This is the 'pricing to win work' model. In other words, pricing to ensure you keep busy. The thinking is price is the only way you can differentiate. This is what is known as a race to the bottom.

OPPORTUNITY COST – WHAT YOU CANNOT SEE

The tradie mindset syndrome frame of thinking results in a focus on what is physically in front of the owner. Focus is fixed on what can be seen – 'Here is a set of plans, or here is a customer in front of me, so I must win this work. I can see it, so I grab it.' You want the work now, often giving no consideration to what are the other potential alternatives – and the potential alternatives that could provide a better return on your investment.

In my experience, very few tradie business owners understand opportunity cost – that is, potential alternatives – due to a lack of confidence. And this lack of confidence is due to their fear of the unknown. If they knock back a job, they cannot see any other new business opportunities. They cannot see what is around the corner, so they think it is better to take the work that is on the table in front of them. Due to a lack of confidence, they incorrectly think, *as long as the team is busy, I can keep things ticking over.* A ticking time bomb more to the point.

Confidence is delivered with planning. Looking forward – through working on business development activities such as developing a sales pipeline forecaster – provides confidence. As the business owner, you know the upcoming months and quarters are signed up with quality clients. Because priority and effort had been placed in business development every week, you can be selective and say no confidently to those clients who are not good for your business.

What is opportunity cost? Simply, it is the loss of other alternatives when one alternative is chosen. This is something most small business owners never consider. Very rarely do they stop to think about what this decision will cost them – not the costs if the project loses money, but rather in terms of other profitable opportunities. Profitable opportunities that will have to be passed up because time and money resources have been committed elsewhere, meaning the business has no more capacity to undertake anything else. As part of the evaluation process, you must stop and think about your alternatives, including the alternative ways to invest resources that are potentially less risky, and potentially more profitable.

TOM THE TRADIE & MR CREATURE

Who is Mr Creature? As introduced in chapter 8, Mr Creature is the type of client that is bad for business. We have all had one at one stage or another. Typically, Mr Creature is someone who always tries to knock the price down, is continually slow to pay, and constantly bargaining to try to get something for nothing. They take up a lot of your time and cost you money in the end.

Here is a common story to explain why, as a business owner, you must always consider what you cannot see. In our story, Tom the Tradie commences a big project for a new client, Mr Creature, that is expected to take six months. Tom plans and allocates his team, his trucks and equipment, along with his personal time and all his mental energy, towards delivering this project. It is the first commercial project he has undertaken and is an important project. Based on his lack of commercial experience, Tom prices the project tightly at $300,000, with no contingency factored in. Tom believes it is a great opportunity to get the 'foot in the door' in a new market that he believes is full of great opportunities.

As the project got underway Tom became fixated with the delivery of the project. He just wanted to get things done. During the early stages of the project, however, Tom did not pay much attention to the fact that Mr Creature was operating in an unprofessional way. Mr Creature's poor planning of trades led to work not being ready on time, poor communication led to mistakes, and changes to the project scope were being made on the run without consultation, leading to confusion.

All these early warning signs were overlooked. Tom was happy to work through the initial issues, totally oblivious to the future negative impact this would create for his business. The following table highlights the impact.

Mr Creature	Tom's problem – feel it now	Tom's raw cost – hidden future impact
Poor planning – work not ready on time	Labour, equipment and materials sitting idle, not productive Stage milestone incomplete and cannot be invoiced	Missed potential revenue for other clients Resources have been paid Cash flow severely impacted due to work not invoiced
Poor communication – mistakes	Reallocate resources to rework Record rework time and materials to be claimed	Cost to redeploy resources Time to calculate claim, submit claim, payment of claim Missed potential revenue Cash flow impacted
Changes to scope – confusion	Reallocate resources to variation Record variation for time and materials to be claimed	Cost to redeploy resources Time to calculate variation, submit variation, payment of variation Missed potential revenue Cash flow impacted

The opportunity cost while Tom has all his resources tied up with Mr Creature is all the other potential alternatives where resources could be allocated. Do not be fooled by the tradie mindset syndrome into thinking being busy is good for business. Do not mistake being busy for being profitable.

Prior to commencing any work for new clients you must conduct research. Speak to people who have worked for them previously, speak to their suppliers. You need to gain a clear picture of who they are prior to committing to work. If the picture developed is of a 'Mr Creature' client, you must avoid them. Stay clear of these clients, because they are not good for business.

THINK MARGIN *NOT* MARK UP TO INCREASE PROFIT

Most of the thousands of tradie business owners who attend my business training sessions think the only way to increase their profit – and, ultimately, their personal financial return – is to work more. The tradie mindset syndrome thinking is focused on working harder, not smarter. Rather than thinking, *How can I do more jobs in a day, in a week, or in a month?* Thinking must be focused on, *How can I generate more profit from each job?* This is using business performance mindset thinking.

Every job you undertake requires you to purchase resources for the job to be completed. These resources can include materials, equipment hire, fees, consultants and sub-contractors. In accounting terms, we label these resources as 'cost of sale' or 'direct costs'. To successfully complete the job, you're required to plan, prepare, order, store and manage all direct costs. This takes time, energy and expertise; all of which needs to be charged to the customer.

To generate more profit when calculating the price of your next job, start thinking in terms of 'gross profit margin', not 'mark up'. When I ask business owners whether mark up is the same as gross profit margin, 90 per cent say yes. This is incorrect. I instruct all my clients to stop using mark up as way of calculating their charge out for direct costs. The following table outlines why.

Using mark up calculation		Using gross profit margin calculation	
Annual material spend	$130,000	Annual material spend	$130,000
Mark up	30%	Gross profit margin	30%
Calculation	130,000 × (1 + 30%)	Calculation	130,000 ÷ (1 − 30%)
Sell price	$169,000	Sell price	$185,714
Gross profit	$39,000	Gross profit	$55,714
Gross profit margin	23%	Gross profit margin	30%
What is good for me? Margin! Delivers an extra $16,714 gross profit			

Using the gross profit margin calculation equals more profit. The example shown in the table clearly illustrates that mark up is not the same as gross profit. Based on the above calculations, an extra $16,714 gross profit was generated from charging out material using the gross profit margin calculation. This gross profit drops straight to your bottom line operating profit. Without doing any more jobs, an extra $16,714 was delivered in profit.

Business owners operating in the business performance mindset understand that the 'power of percentages' is the true secret to increasing their financial return, and they have the confidence to take advantage of them. Using the example shown in the preceding table, if the gross profit margin was increased from 30 per cent to 35 per cent, an extra $6,842 would be generated in gross profit.

These calculations highlight that you do not have to work more to increase profit.

Score Your Business: How many business owners price for profit?

The 'Score Your Business' assessment asked trade service and construction business owners about the level to which business break-even is used to determine pricing for profit.

Business owners who know their pricing for profit

The assessment asked owners, 'Do you know your current business "break-even point" and required "charge-out rate" to ensure you generate profit? (What is your required charge out rate to generate profit, considering margins, the cost to operate the business and actual billable hours?)'. Responses are shown in the following table.

Turnover	Know pricing for profit	As % of category
Less than $300K	79	32%
$300K–$600K	45	40%
$600K–$1M	24	41%
More than $1M	19	38%
Total	**167**	**36%**

Level of satisfaction based on pricing for profit.

Satisfaction levels based on having, or not having, a pricing for profit model are shown in the following table.

Turnover	Know pricing for profit and satisfied achieving personal goals	Don't know pricing for profit and satisfied achieving personal goals
Less than $300K	*38%*	*25%*
$300K–$600K	*27%*	*22%*
$600K–$1M	*21%*	*17%*
More than $1M	*37%*	*16%*
Total	**32%**	**23%**

The key point here is for business owners with turnover greater than $1,000,000, 37 per cent of those who know their price for profit are satisfied, compared to only 16 per cent of those who don't know their price for profit. Accurately calculating what a business must charge to guarantee profit is difficult for most business owners. This is due to the fact that most have poor financial record keeping, lacking detail and often missing information. Therefore, calculating price for profit is placed in the 'too-hard basket', and is never done. Alternatively, business owners use incorrect calculations, leading to significant financial losses.

Your takeaways

1. Identify your Mr Creature clients and sack them now – have the confidence to say no.

2. Remove mark up from all your pricing calculations – calculate your direct cost price using the gross profit margin calculation.

3. Increase your gross profit margin to increase your operating profit – work less and earn more.

CHAPTER 19

Educate *not* sell

RACE TO THE BOTTOM

Remember the definition of insanity from earlier in the book? Basically, insanity is doing the same thing repeatedly but expecting a different result. A lot of tradie business owners come to me frustrated because they are constantly missing out on jobs based on price. They ask how they can stop competing solely on price. They are sick and tired of working hard for people who do not appreciate the value in the quality of products and services they deliver. They are over being busy all the time, yet still not achieving their personal financial goals.

Operating in the 'competing on price cycle' year on year is depressing, demotivating and unsustainable. In this 'race to the bottom', no tradie can win. No tradie wins in a race to the lowest price, especially when considering the business operating landscape where competition is fierce, customer expectation is extreme, and compliance costs are constantly increasing.

So how do you stop competing on price? Firstly, you must understand the internet age has forever changed the way you do business. Your customers now have access to information about the market you service, including market pricing, your competitors and your previous customers' feedback. This results in your customers being well informed from the start.

Customer expectations are high from the very first point of communication they have with your business. Business owners can no longer expect to win a 'profitable' job by simply submitting a quote with limited or missing information, no follow-up, and delivered after the date the customer expected to receive it.

BRING YOUR 'A-GAME' – REMOVE PRICE FROM THE CONVERSATION

For tradie business owners wanting to remove price from the conversation, the first thing I do is to review their current proposal documentation and process – and the common message I see here is 'me, me, me'. The proposal documentation is all about the tradie business – how many years it has been operating, how many tradies employed, what licences and insurances it holds, and what Australian Standards it meets. It is all about me.

When I ask how long has it been since the proposal documentation was reviewed and updated, the common response is three or five years ago, or never. In other words, lazy, 'Other-Game' practices. To break the competing on price cycle you must change your thinking and therefore your actions. You must bring your 'A-Game' and think educate. Think, *How can I educate my prospect to understand the true value I will deliver?* This can relate to the quality of your job management, materials, workmanship, equipment, warranties and/ or after-sales service. You must unlock all the hidden value that is not visible in the price.

Increasing your profit, and long-term sustainability, is not about selling. It's about establishing trust, rapport and value creation for your clients. For me personally, I don't want to do business with someone who wants to sell their products or services by bombarding me with information. I want to communicate with someone who empathises with my problem and who can solve my problems.

Engage with me, communicate with me, add value to my business, solve my problems, create opportunity for me, educate me and inform me, but don't try to sell me – it won't work. An attempt to sell me insults my intelligence and wastes my time. Nobody likes to be sold to; however, most people like to be helped.

Become the problem expert

Many tradies operating in the tradie mindset syndrome make the mistake of attempting to stand for everything. They want to do everything, and they want to be all things to all people. The problem is when you attempt to be known for everything, you don't become known for anything. You will never be known as an expert in solving a specific problem, placing you in the race to the bottom competing on price cycle.

To engage, inform and solve problems you must understand the type of person you want to help. As discussed in chapter 17, you must become the expert in understanding what is important to your ideal client.

For example, if you are targeting busy professional couples living in the inner city, clear and consistent communication is extremely important for this typically time-poor client. Price is not as important as being professional and on time. Once you understand what is important to your ideal client, you must then effectively educate that you are the expert in solving their problem.

Educate leads to expert

Experts in all fields are very good at educating their customers. As a result of focusing on education, the business becomes positioned as the expert in the field. Experts understand that the first problem faced by their ideal client when making any buying decision relates to what information they need to make an educated buying decision.

Start educating your ideal client by communicating:

- how you understand their actual problems

- the pros of your solution versus the cons of a solution based only on price – use photo evidence and case studies

- the positive return on investment for your solution – calculate the payback period of upfront capital purchases based on factoring in savings relating to running costs and ongoing maintenance expenses

- the peace of mind from choosing quality products backed by warranties and service guarantees.

Score Your Business:
How many business owners know what makes them different?

The 'Score Your Business' assessment asked the 466 trade service and construction business owners about what makes them different.

Business owners who know what makes them different

The assessment asked owners, 'Do you know what makes you different from your competitors – why you are unique? (Do you survey your customers' level of satisfaction to understand what makes your client happy to use you over your competitor?)' The following table summarises responses.

Turnover	Know what makes them different	As % of category
Less than $300K	122	50%
$300K–$600K	64	57%
$600K–$1M	37	63%
More than $1M	25	50%
Total	**248**	**53%**

The table shows over 50 per cent of business owners understand what makes them unique and why customers choose them over their competitors.

Level of satisfaction based on knowing what makes them different

The following table summarises business owners' satisfaction levels from knowing their unique selling points.

Turnover	Know what makes them different and satisfied achieving personal goals	Don't know what makes them different and satisfied achieving personal goals
Less than $300K	34%	24%
$300K–$600K	23%	25%
$600K–$1M	24%	9%
More than $1M	36%	12%
Total	30%	22%

The key points here are as follows:

- As the business increases in turnover, the number of business owners who are satisfied without knowing what makes them different plummets to only 12 per cent. This highlights the importance of, as you grow, understanding what unique problems you solve so you can educate those profile target customers who must understand the value delivered.

- Too often as a business grows the owner loses sight of what made them different in the first place due to trying to be all things to all people. This is a warning sign of potentially 'growing broke', where lots of the wrong type of work is being done.

Your takeaways

1. Identify what information your ideal client needs to know and understand so they can make an educated buying decision – and understand how you can assist your client in making the right choice.

2. Update all your marketing and proposal collateral to effectively educate your ideal customer – clearly articulate the value your solution will deliver.

3. Educate, educate, educate …

Case study:
Educating your customer

Solar and sustainability become the buzz words in the electricity market during the 2000s, and the market soon became inundated with solar hot water solutions and installers. The whole area became confusing for the home owner, with the most common question being, 'So what is the best solar hot water system for my home?'

With the installation market becoming very competitive, price became the only area where most businesses were able to differentiate their products and services. Most businesses failed to educate their potential customer in even the basics of what to look for when making a buying decision.

During this period we worked with a number of solar hot water installation businesses to assist in educating their market, not selling to their market. The key areas presented to potential clients included:

- *Articulation of the problem:* We understand this is a large purchase item for the home and consideration needs to be given to the location, use and hot water volume required from the system to ensure ongoing running cost savings are delivered.

- *Articulation of why Australian Standards:* As per the Australian Standards, we install UV lagging on the flow and return (yes, this is more expensive, but it maintains system efficiency to reduce running costs), we install a tempering valve (yes, expensive, but this reduces the risk of scalding), and we install quality systems (which are tried and tested for the local environment), all of which provides the home owner with peace of mind.

- *Evidence of credibility:* Provide photos of professional installations for the recommended solution. Provide client testimonials.

- *Calculate the financial return on investment:* Provide a payback period when the initial investment will be recovered and then ongoing savings gained thereafter. This is based on the annual savings in running costs the new solution will deliver. Provide client case studies.

- *Highlight the warranty and service:* Provide peace of mind in knowing that a quality solution has been installed that is supported with warranty and local service.

The preceding points were presented in a professionally bound expression of interest proposal document. Conversion rates and profit increased through educating those clients who believed the solution offered solved their problem and delivered great value.

CHAPTER 20

Predict your future

KNOW YOUR SCOREBOARD

What separates the most successful business operators from the rest? They check their scoreboard – in other words, their stats and their industry trends – to predict their future. Why? Because they want to guarantee their success. As speaker and author Keith Cunningham notes, 'What gets measured gets done. What gets measured gets managed. What gets measured and reported improves exponentially.'

As a business owner, you operate in a 12-month season, known as the financial year. During the season, the score and all the key areas that drive performance must be regularly reviewed – on a daily or weekly basis – against the required goal or target.

The key areas requiring recording, measuring and reporting will include number of leads and conversions, sales, individual productivity relating to billable hours capacity, individual job gross profitability, break-even point and business profitability.

From my experience training, consulting and coaching thousands of trade business owners, very few businesses take the time to stop and accurately check their score. A lot of business owners will go through the whole season without once checking their score – often only reviewing their score some 18 to 24 months after the start of the season.

Most owners will say that they don't have the time to check the score. The real reason is that, due to poor and inaccurate recording of operating data, the scoreboard doesn't make sense. Therefore, most owners consider reviewing the score a waste of time. Here is the tradie mindset syndrome again – rather than fix the problem by improving the quality of data recorded, the head is placed in the sand to ignore the score all together.

Simply, all focus is being placed on the job (the activity) and no attention is paid to the result (the scorecard). When all your focus is placed on the activity, meaning getting things done, you can't make 'educated business decisions' regarding the future. All decisions are simply 'guessing'. When it comes to business, guessing is gambling – resulting in poor choices, which lead to lost time and lost money. For the trade business owner this means being very busy, but not getting ahead financially.

DO AS SPORTS TEAMS DO

How many sporting teams play a game without looking at the scoreboard to see how they are performing? How many sporting teams play a game without analysing the key statistics that drive performance? None. Sporting teams understand that the scoreboard and the statistics do not lie. They are the facts that direct where time, energy and effort must be focused at training during the week to improve performance in the next game. Win or lose, performance improvements can be made. Sporting teams understand the result of the game cannot be controlled, and that performance is the only controllable.

Applying the same logic to business, these are the key business performance areas in your scoreboard you should be reviewing:

- *Leads and conversions:* Which marketing is generating the most leads resulting in the highest conversion rate with the highest profitability per job?

- *Work type profitability:* Which work delivers gross profit and which work costs money?

- *Customer type profitability:* Which customers deliver gross profit and which customers cost money?

- *Individual productivity:* Which team members deliver the most billable hours and which team members deliver the lowest billable hours?

- *Deployment of resources:* Based on a percentage of turnover, how efficient is investment relating to direct and indirect employees, training, tools and equipment, insurance, vehicles and operating the office.

How often do you review these areas?

Harder not smarter

Recording, reporting and analysing the scoreboard is the foundation of operating in the business performance mindset. It is the base for making educated business decisions – where, before saying yes, all potential benefits and potential risks are considered.

If as a trade business owner you don't look at your scoreboard to analyse performance, you're destined to live within the tradie mindset syndrome of working harder not smarter. You're stuck with the following:

- Each time the phone rings, it is important and urgent – just like a fire chief, you *must* rush off and put out fires.

- You're always busy, all the time – everything is completed in a rush at the last minute.
- You say yes to all work – never say no.
- You never get ahead financially – always struggling to pay bills at tax time.
- You have no time for holidays – life has become work.
- No motivation, no passion, no bright future!

THE POTENTIAL FUTURE – FAILURE

As I have noted throughout this book, the preceding picture of living with tradie mindset syndrome is not what you envisioned when you started your business with great enthusiasm and optimism. But the reality that eventuates for most tradie business owners means that, based on my research, only 26 per cent are satisfied they are achieving their personal goals. This relates to achieving their desired lifestyle and personal wealth, while at the same time reducing hours worked and stress levels.

My research findings show the main reason for business failure comes down to the business owner's lack of financial awareness – meaning the business owner fails to review and/or interpret their scoreboard.

My own research, backed up by that found in many business publications, shows over 50 per cent of businesses fail due to:

- *Lack of planning:* Poor direction due to minimal reflection on past wins and losses. Lack of learning from past mistakes.
- *Poor record-keeping:* Inaccurate and missing critical business information results in an inaccurate scoreboard.
- *Lack of financial awareness:* Due to inaccurate and limited information reported, owners are unable to interpret or understand business performance.

Predict your future

To ensure you do not become a statistic, as the business leader you must make potentially tough decisions – such as letting staff go and cutting long-term clients. These decisions are made easier when time has been invested in considering the future to predict performance and outcomes. With a clear understanding of what decisions need to be made to ensure the desired outcome, action can be taken swiftly.

With no plan, prediction, forecast, budget, goal (or whatever you may call it), you have no reason to report and measure your scorecard. With no plan you have no reason to accurately record all your financial information, and by default you have no financial intelligence.

We set all our clients up with the 'CUBE – My Business Intelligence' software platform to predict performance and drive measurement of outcomes, in real time. The CUBE empowers business owners with the financial intelligence to make the tough, educated decisions relating to the success of the business. The success refers to being a sustainable business, delivering profit and cash flow.

The CUBE breaks down all revenue, direct costs, overhead investments and capacity into units that can be recorded, measured and acted upon. This delivers clear performance expectations, driving accountability throughout the business.

Through predicting future outcomes, priority tasks are easily identified – telling you what must to be acted on today to maintain desired performance levels. This then becomes a continual cycle of predict, prioritise and act, as shown in the following figure.

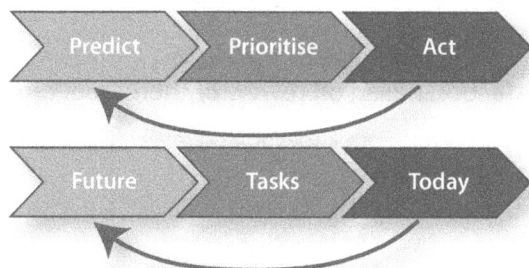

Score Your Business:
How many business owners review their score?

The 'Score Your Business' assessment asked trade service and construction business owners whether they had a scoreboard and, if so, how many review their score.

Business owners who review their score monthly

The research asked, 'Do you generate a Profit & Loss report and review performance against your budget monthly? (Are you on track with sales, cost of sale, gross profit, labour, expense categories, net profit?)' The following table outlines responses.

Turnover	Owners who review their score monthly	As % of category
Less than $300K	47	19%
$300K–$600K	34	30%
$600K–$1M	26	44%
More than $1M	24	48%
Total	131	28%

The results show that only 28 per cent of business owners review their score monthly. Therefore, most business owners do not understand what areas are working and what requires improvement. Without reviewing the score, the owner will never be able to consistently improve performance. The score highlights the facts relating to how effective the owner is at managing the business.

Level of satisfaction based on review of their score monthly

Owner satisfaction levels from knowing and reviewing their scoreboard are shown in the following table.

Turnover	Who review their score monthly and satisfied achieving personal goals	Don't review their score monthly and satisfied achieving personal goals
Less than $300K	43%	26%
$300K–$600K	35%	19%
$600K–$1M	27%	12%
More than $1M	29%	19%
Total	**35%**	**23%**

The point to note here is that the key to scoring business performance relates to the information being accurate, in full, and on time. The information recorded and reported in the scorecard must be 100 per cent accurate, with all information recorded in detail, and, importantly, must have data relating to the current time period.

Your takeaways

1. Create your 'scoreboard' – break down your financial and performance data so it can be easily recorded and reported.

2. Invest time to review scoreboard weekly and monthly – measure your performance against your goals to guarantee you are making 'profit' and not just being 'busy'.

Case study: Understanding the story of business

Let's examine a business turnaround success story where the directors, initially, were 'guessing' and flying by the seat of their pants when making business decisions. Originally in the business, all focus was placed on sales and getting the job done, with no attention given to understanding the financial story of the business. With a complete change of focus, the business then became one where the directors based all decision-making on profitability and detailed financial information.

The company was Fit Services Australia (Commercial Maintenance & Cleaning), and its directors, Craig Markham and Bryan Fletcher (former NRL star & Fox Sports commentator), had no problem selling. They were fantastic at generating a lot of sales, and over a three-year period grew turnover to $8 million. As a result, everyone in the business became very busy getting through the increased work load. This dramatically increased the pressure on their operations team to deliver the work, and the administration team to process the work.

Problem

Due to the increased demands and lack of systems, the management team got caught up in the day-to-day running of the business. They were constantly reactive to all situations and putting out fires. Financial reporting was lacking, leading to no accountability and no clear understanding of how they were performing. Because the focus was on selling and getting the work done (the activity), they were unaware that the business was struggling in terms of profit and cash flow (the scorecard). A lot of resources had been allocated with no control.

Solution

With the management team, we conducted a complete review of the business. We identified, due to a lack of systems and processes, the financial reporting was inaccurate and missed critical data.

We implemented the following:

- detailed account coding breaking down and itemising of sales, cost of sale and overheads
- development and adoption of 'financial scorecard', measuring customer sales, gross profit, and margins by work type and department
- accountability across all departments – clear performance goals
- cash flow forecasting – daily management of bank transactions
- monthly management performance reviews – reviewing financial performance line by line, measuring actual results versus budget/ forecast results, and critical analysis
- customer profiling – identifying 'A' clients based on payment terms, gross profit and referrals generated; this led to the sacking of 'Mr Creature' clients.

Outcome

At the 12-month mark after implementation, the results were as follows:

- sales reduced – new 'educated' sales decision-making became based on profit *not* turnover
- profit increased by 300 per cent
- cash flow improved dramatically
- management team had 'peace of mind' knowing they were in control of the business.

The financial intelligence delivered through knowing the scoreboard and analysing performance with trading history enabled accurate prediction of future performance – making decision-making easy.

CHAPTER 21

Attracting and retaining great people

YOUR NUMBER ONE PRIORITY

For Richard Branson and his Virgin businesses, people are his priority. Virgin has a culture of making it fun, breaking all the rules and empowering their team members. This attracts a certain type of individual to work for the company. People considering working there, for example, may think *I am the type of person who likes to follow rules, likes to follow the pack and is conservative, so there is a high possibility I will not fit in. Therefore, I am not attracted to work for Virgin.* People who think the opposite, of course, are highly attracted to working for Virgin. Branson has created a very clear personality for his Virgin brand. It speaks out, says, 'This is what we believe in and if you believe the same come and have fun with us'. As Branson says, 'Create the kind of workplace and company culture that will attract great talent. If you hire brilliant people, they will make work feel more like play.'

Think about this for your business. Richard Branson also states that by putting the employee first, 'the customer effectively comes first by default and, in the end, the shareholder comes first by default as well'. Have you ever considered putting your team first?

I know from my own experience operating a plumbing business, I often became focused on getting the job done to satisfy the customer. In doing so, I would often neglect the team, simply assuming they would turn up to get the job done. I didn't think about how I could make the work environment better for them. I didn't ask for feedback on how we could do things better. At the time, I knew no better – I was operating in the 'tradie mindset syndrome', with a sole focus on getting the job done so we could move onto the next job.

IT IS ALL ABOUT THE PEOPLE

As a business owner, manager and leader, your success is based on your ability to attract and retain great people with great talent. I see most business owners lacking the understanding, and confidence, in building a team full of individuals with the right capability, great attitude and, importantly, belief in the 'way we do it here'.

I am sure it comes as no surprise that at the time of writing we are in the middle of a labour skill shortage. Through my travels conducting national business training for trade business owners, a problem I continually hear is the lack of suitably qualified and motivated candidates. This feedback is backed up by 2016 statistics published by the Australian Government, stating construction trades workers account for the largest number of occupations in shortage, with only 55 per cent of vacancies filled.

Dominate your market – your competitive advantage

If you are looking for a competitive advantage and are serious about dominating your market this year, next year and beyond, you must ask yourself this big question today: 'How do I prepare the business to attract and retain talented people?' To dominate your market, you must always deliver on your customer promise, and you must always provide a consistent customer experience at every interaction. For this to happen, you require a great team who are motivated and inspired to follow you.

To build a great team who consistently deliver quality performance, day in, day out, you must change your tradie mindset syndrome thinking. First, stop thinking that the only thing your team care about is the pay check. Yes, the pay check is obviously important, but this will not inspire someone to follow you. Second, stop thinking your business would perform better if the team were better. If your team is underperforming, it is because of you. You designed the team based on your previous action and inaction. Remember – you need to be accountable, so own it.

Now let's prepare your business to dominate your market.

INSPIRE – WHAT IS YOUR PURPOSE?

The new generation of employees, along with talented individuals, want to be inspired through being part of something bigger than themselves. They want to follow a leader who inspires and empowers them to take ownership. As outlined in part II of the book ('Stage 1: Clarity'), having a clear purpose sets clear expectations. For example, promising customers 'peace of mind, knowing that one call and it is done', will inspire your team to make it happen to ensure the customer doesn't ring twice.

A clear purpose and promise sets performance expectations for all to follow. Importantly, if a team member doesn't believe in your purpose, it is time to part ways – this is non-negotiable. One in, all in. This is where 'hire slow, fire fast' is important. Take your time to find and select the right individual, which means starting the recruitment process well before you have work for them. Take your time to induct, train and immerse the individual into the 'way we do it here'. If after this process you find they are the wrong fit, remove them from the business quickly, and start the process again.

Autonomy through automation

In chapter 16 I outlined that one of the business owner's primary areas of focus needs to be on developing the appropriate systems and processes that support the team.

As the leader, you need to 100 per cent have trust in your team. Even if you have good intentions, jumping in to micromanage situations demonstrates to your team an obvious lack of trust. You must get out of the way and allow your team to learn and develop through experience. A lot of business owners need to understand it is not all about them and their own self-importance.

Great talent want autonomy so they can get on with it. They don't want to be micromanaged or have to ask how to do things. You must invest both time and money in developing the required systems and processes that will automate tasks. Automation allows you to effectively delegate responsibility. You want to be known as a leader who invests in systems that support all team members to be successful in their roles. Be known as a leader who develops people with the skills, principles and attitude be successful in life, long after they have left your business.

Mastery through training

As a leader who wants to develop a high-performing team, it is critical you invest in specific training, both in-house and external. It amazes me when a business owner states their most important resource is their team, but when I ask them what they're budgeting to invest in the team's training, the answer is zero. To continually develop your team, you must invest time, energy and money. A great team will not just happen.

For talented individuals, becoming an expert or gaining mastery of a specific skill is very important – as is using specialised equipment, implementing a solution or delivering a program. These individuals want to grow and expand their skill and knowledge. They are not content to drift through the day to day, spinning on the same spot; they want to progress forward.

For you to retain great talent, they need to understand the larger plan for them. Don't treat them like a mushroom – keeping them in the dark and expecting them to flourish. It won't happen.

GET STARTED

Preparation for creating a great team must start today – this is not a one-off project, this must become part your DNA in terms of how your business operates daily. This all starts with you as the business owner and leader – you must believe in this.

The progressive businesses that are doing this well are gaining massive competitive advantage. These progressive businesses have great talent lining up, wanting an opportunity to work for them, offering great choices in candidates. Individuals want to work for these businesses, so they do not have to continually increase pay rates to retain individuals. Importantly, customer satisfaction increases because the entire team believe in what they do. Start inspiring today – it starts with you.

Find what motivates your team

If you're serious about dominating your market, I recommend reading Dan Pink's *Drive: The Surprising Truth About What Motivates Us*. For any job that requires thought, creativity or problem-solving, Pink doesn't recommend a focus on concrete rewards (such as pay and bonuses) and punishments.

Of course, construction and trade service employee tasks require thought, creativity and problem-solving, on a day-to-day basis, so Pink's ideas can be applied to your business and employees. Pink outlines three elements you must provide to employees who are faced with these types of tasks:

- *Autonomy:* The desire to direct their own life.
- *Mastery:* The urge to make progress and get better at something that matters.
- *Purpose:* The yearning to do what they do in the service of something larger than themselves.

Opportunity to change lives

As a business owner, you have a great opportunity to positively affect people's lives through your leadership and teachings. You have the opportunity to instil life principles and values that will ensure the individual's success long after they have left your business. This is the sign of a great leader, one who leaves a positive legacy with all those they come into contact with through instilling belief and confidence.

As a leader, building a great team is not simply about results. It has everything to do with how leaders evolve on their personal journey and how this shapes their performance relating to morals, ethics, empathy, resilience and persistence.

Your takeaways

1. Invest in systems and processes to automate tasks – support individuals to be successful in their roles.

2. Invest in training to develop your team – support individuals to be masters in their roles.

3. Think what you need to start doing today to guarantee talented people are lining up to work for you in the future.

PART V

Stage 4: Connection

Success achieved over a sustained period is based on forming and nurturing industry and community connections. And success over a long period of time is based on the quality of your connections, relationships and partnerships. In my experience, going it alone is very, very, very difficult. Why? Because by going it alone, you miss out on leverage.

Connecting and forming relationships with the right partners provides your business with opportunities to potentially access client lists, increase credibility and increase financial returns on investment – all because of leverage. Leverage is delivered when organisations with the same vison and beliefs form win–win partnerships, creating value for customers and the community.

CHAPTER 22

Partnerships lead to opportunity

IT IS ALL ABOUT BELIEF AND VALUES

Thus far, the Blueprint for Success methodology has outlined the following stages:

- *Stage 1 – Clarity:* Gaining a clear understanding of the 'way we do it here' and a clear vision of what needs to be achieved.

- *Stage 2 – Control:* Implementing business intelligence and process to predict performance and create a blueprint that will guarantee future success.

- *Stage 3 – Confidence:* Making decisions that will position the business to attract great team members, great clients and great partners.

The fourth and final stage on the Blueprint for Success is Connection. With a clear vision, a repeatable blueprint for success and the confidence to make it happen, Connection is what will propel your business forward. Connection relates to the power of partnerships and leverage.

Partnerships are often misunderstood, or completely over-looked, as a way for a business to build credibility or access potential clients. Why? It all comes back to mindset and thinking. The tradie mindset syndrome has the business owner thinking they can do it alone, and that they do not need assistance.

From my experience, partnerships are the most powerful way to build a business. Partnerships open a vast array of potential opportunities, especially if both parties are adding equal value to the relationship. A notable example of this is my partnership with Telstra via developing the Trades Assist work management software platform. This partnership is based on each party delivering value. I am providing value to Telstra through providing industry credibility and knowledge via the Blueprint for Success framework and The CUBE business intelligence software. And Telstra are providing me with value through providing a channel to communicate my message and belief to a large, engaged audience. (Refer to chapter 16 for more on this platform.)

FORMING WIN–WIN PARTNERSHIPS

For me this area is all about win–win partnerships. Win–win partnerships can only exist if both parties have the same belief and values system. As former president of the Philippines Benigno Aquino III highlighted, 'Strategic partnership is based on a shared set of values'. The Reece and Cube Performance partnership (refer to chapter 9) works because we have the same values – focus on customer satisfaction, continual improvement and adding value. For this reason, the partnership works.

Most business partnerships never deliver win–win results due to differing visions and values. I receive a lot of feedback from business owners who say something like, 'Jonesy I have tried partnerships but they have always been a waste of time'. To this, I ask them whether they started with shared vision and values, and whether they give the partnership enough time.

This is where bringing your 'A-Game' to researching is invaluable. To save time, energy and lots of potential pain, before you make the call to a potential partner you must research. Review online information, check reviews, speak with other tradies who have worked for them, and speak with customers who have engaged them. You will quickly gain a clear picture. If your business is all about delivering high-quality, long-term solutions and your research into a potential partner uncovers they are all about low-quality quick fixes, you can quickly put a red line through them. It will never work.

BE COMMITTED AND RESILIENT

Finding a partner with the same vision and values doesn't guarantee success. To formulate the agreed strategy and process, and then to implement, review, modify and go again, all takes time and commitment. Every partnership has a settling period. At times in the early stages both parties may question the validity of the partnership. Is this worth it? When will the value be realised?

During the early stages of implementing the Blueprint for Success training program with Reece (covered in chapter 9), we had to revise the structure and format to deliver the desired results. If both parties were not committed to the vision, the partnership could have easily become all too hard, and pushed down the priority list. It took commitment to push through.

Do not expect things to run smoothly. Expect tough times, especially in the early stages. Invest time to review, discuss and modify all aspects of the partnership. Often the tougher the initial stages, the more fruitful the relationship in the long term.

Take advantage of the power of leverage

Business owners must think leverage. Think about how you can leverage your marketing investment, your time, your systems, your team and your intellectual property. Leverage ultimately opens up opportunities that potentially would not have been realised. (The case study at the end of this chapter expands on this idea.)

Your takeaways

1. Identify which other industry suppliers and providers are currently servicing your ideal customer that can increase your reach – research their vision, values and goals.

2. Select an appropriate potential partner to build a win–win relationship with – and communicate how partnering with you will increase the value delivered to their customer.

3. Stay committed to the partnership – you must invest to build the relationship; it will not just happen.

Case study:
The power of leverage

In early 2000s I was director of a solar hot water installation company. The company's vision was to provide the best short-term and long-term solution for home owners. We valued informing home owners how to make an educated buying decision when it came to purchasing solar hot water. We realised, however, we needed to partner with a manufacturer that could provide brand recognition and credibility, technical expertise and support, and the supply to guarantee delivery.

The pitch

Rheem was our chosen partner. At the first meeting, we pitched our vision, promise and values. They were in. Our beliefs were aligned, and Rheem understood that by investing in the partnership to assist our success, they would also win – a win–win relationship.

Outcomes

The outcomes were as follows:

- *Leveraging marketing resources:* Collaborating with Rheem to develop a 12-month marketing strategy was key to gaining market awareness. The defined strategy included local newspaper advertising across multiple targeted locations, exhibiting at trade shows and industry events, and offering seasonal promotions. All collateral was co-branded, and the investment was split. The Rheem partnership leveraged our marketing spend, increasing exposure and awareness.

- *Gaining market credibility and expertise:* By becoming a Rheem preferred installer, we received the latest technical training to ensure we were educated in the pros and cons for all solar hot water systems across all environments and applications. Based on the detailed running costs Rheem provided, we developed a sophisticated return on investment model. This was communicated in simple terms to the home owner, educating them on how reducing long-term running costs would pay back their investment in a solar hot water system. Through leveraging Rheem's brand and expertise, we gained market credibility.

- *Adding customer value:* As part of the Rheem partnership, we could add value to the home owner's purchase. This included offering increased warranty periods on selected systems and 24-hour priority service. As a result of the partnership, the home owner was able to make an educated decision as to what was the best solution for their situation, providing peace of mind, both in the short and long term.

CHAPTER 23

Be the key person of influence

BECOMING THE 'GO-TO' IN YOUR MARKET

When a leader has clarity in what they want, is always in control while achieving remarkable success, and is constantly pitching their vision for the greater good of the industry, people stop and listen. These types of leaders are the thought leaders of their industry, and they can inspire change that will disrupt industry. Look at leaders such as Henry Ford, Bill Gates, Steve Jobs and Elon Musk – all industry disrupters who changed (or change) the way industry and people go about their lives.

A key person of influence in any market is recognised as an industry leader. These leaders are ahead of the game, and are ahead of their competitors through continually operating on the cutting edge of innovation to shape the way the industry operates. The key person of influence is well connected with individuals and industry bodies that have the ability and resources to enact change.

All key people of influence are inspirational. At every opportunity, they will communicate their vision of a better future for their industry and all industry stakeholders. With industry credibility, they become the 'go-to' person in the market. Rather than having to seek out opportunities, the opportunities come to them.

A business owner who is perceived as a person of influence has a consistent flow of ideal, quality client leads knocking on their door. Conversion rates are high because they are seeking you out. Profit is high because you are not competing with the market – clients are already educated in the value that will be delivered.

In the context of your business and industry, who are the key people of influence? Think what they are doing that positions them as the 'go-to' in your market. Who are they partnering with to leverage expertise and networks? Think about how you can be positioned as the key person of influence within your market. It all starts in the mind with believing it is possible.

Community, connection and investment

When a business successfully stands out from its competitors and can deliver consistent profit, the business owners have the opportunity to be connected with and invest back into their community. Therefore, I believe it is every business owner's duty to be successful in creating a sustainable business. The end in mind for every business owner should include giving back to their community. This can be simply through providing sustainable employment and personal development opportunities for their employees.

When a business struggles to deliver profit, long-term survival is limited. The negative impact on the community when a business fails is huge. The cost to the community flows through to suppliers not being paid and employees not being paid entitlements – potentially flowing through to personal bankruptcy, personal relationship breakdowns and health problems, to name a few. No-one wants a business to fail.

Be the change you want

Key people of influence do not sit back to wait for industry change to happen. They actively go out to make the required change happen. They excitedly follow their passion, and this excitement then rubs off on others, building momentum for change to happen.

From your view of your industry right now, what positive change would you like to see happen? What are you passionate about? What potential change would be beneficial to all in your industry? If you truly believe in something, follow it. Don't wait for others to make change happen; you must be the change agent.

Importantly, you must identify who can help you on your journey. This is where partnering with organisations with the same vision and beliefs is critical. As a business owner, going it alone to build your influence within your industry is next to impossible. You need partners who provide the necessary support, expertise and resources you can leverage to make it happen.

Your takeaways

1. Identify the key people of influence shaping your industry.

2. Outline the changes you would like to see happen in your industry – what will improve the lives of all?

3. Make change happen – don't sit back and wait.

CHAPTER 24

'Done great'

YOUR STORY

The aim of this book is to assist business owners in creating their own business success stories. Every business person appreciates positive accolades from their industry peers and close friends, and nothing is more satisfying than when people who you respect notice all your hard work is paying off. It is especially satisfying when you pleasantly surprise those who initially doubted your ability.

In life you often only get one chance to create your story. I hope in some way this book inspires you to let go of all your fears and doubts, to change your thinking to what is possible and, importantly, to get started on your story.

You have an amazing opportunity to create a great story, so do not let this pass. Don't let yourself get down for not having achieved what you had planned for your current stage of life. The great thing in life is that if you are unhappy with your current circumstance, it doesn't have to be your destination. You don't have to live there. It is just a stopover on your journey.

Keep the seasons in mind

When creating your business success story, you must always take into account the seasons. Acclaimed personal development guru Jim Rohn stated that you cannot change the seasons; you can only change yourself. Rohn explains why it is important for business owners to prepare for the seasons ahead.

First, you must learn how to survive the winter. Some winters are long and some are short. During winter, you must become stronger, wiser and better to ensure you survive next winter. It is important to think positively, because winters do not last forever. Winter for your business may relate to increased competition, reduced demand or tough economic times leading to a reduction in development investment.

Second is spring. In this season, you must take advantage of the day and grab the opportunity for a new beginning, and the opportunity to turn things around. Spring is a short season and is also planting season, so you must hurry. You need to pick the right seeds, along with the right location and right nourishment. Just as life is short, you must learn to appreciate the opportunities that are presented. Only a small window of time is open, so you must be prepared to take it. In business during the spring, you must be planting the seeds relating to growing business development opportunities, growing win–win partnerships, and growing a high-performance culture within your team.

The third season is summer. This is a time to nourish new life and protect it like a father, as you wait for opportunities to present from the planted seeds. This is also a time to beware of the thief in your mind that is after your promise. Do not become a victim of yourself through negative thoughts such as, *I cannot do it because there are too many obstacles.* This is the time to maintain belief in your ability and remain focused on your goals.

The fourth season is autumn – time to harvest and to reap what you have sowed. The more intelligent the work invested, the greater the rewards. For all in due season, your harvest will come if you are patient enough to wait.

Business owners who have created success stories understand the seasons. They understand that tough times do not last forever, just as good times will not last forever. Successful people are always preparing for the season ahead.

TOM'S CHANGE STORY

The example of Tom the Tradie has come up a few times throughout this book. Let's now fast-track to see how Tom travelled on his journey.

Five years ago while catching up with Frank, an old colleague, Tom had a vision of what he was destined to become, and he didn't like what he saw. Tom and Frank started their apprenticeships at the same time, and they had both started their own businesses seven years earlier.

Tom realised every time he caught up with Frank the conversation was always negative. They were always the victims. They never took responsibility for why their businesses were continually on life support. Blame was directed at their customers, their team, their suppliers, the government and so on. They were to blame for why they were busy all the time yet still not achieving their personal goals. In these conversations, Tom could hear his former boss speaking, the boss who became a broke, bitter and lonely old man. Tom always swore he would never be like his old boss and this realisation scared him.

Once Frank left, Tom went and looked at himself in the mirror. He knew he needed to change his thinking towards business. He knew he needed to change his environment and the people he hung out with. He knew he needed to own his current failings and accept 100 per cent responsibility.

Tom invested in a self-development journey. Firstly, he changed his thinking from tradie mindset syndrome to business performance mindset. This immediately changed the way he viewed his business and, importantly, made him change his behaviours. He fully adopted the Blueprint for Success methodology, successfully implementing clarity, control, confidence and connection within his business.

For Tom's next catch-up with Frank, four years had passed since the last. Frank opened the conversation, and as he began to talk Tom thought to himself that nothing had changed for Frank in four years. He was living in groundhog day. He was still the victim, still enslaved to his job with a poor quality of life, and still not happy within himself.

After a period of this talk, Frank asked Tom how he was going. Tom explained that in the four years since their last catch-up he had changed his thinking regarding accountability. This had led to a massive change in fortune. The business was now operated under management, with the team operating the systems and processes Tom had implemented and now managed a smaller base of more profitable and valuable customers. The business was now attracting talented people and profitable customers. Tom's personal investment plan was growing building future wealth and, importantly, Tom was enjoying lots and lots of great family time, sharing travels around the world. Life was great.

Frank said to Tom, 'Mate, you have done great.' As he said this, Frank's mind was racing, trying to work out how this change happened. He was happy for Tom, but hearing his story made him feel despair in not having made any change to his life. Frank's wife and kids were always asking to travel overseas, with his standard response being no time and no money. Frank was feeling as though he was letting down his family and himself, feeling guilty about hav-ing invested so much time into the business yet with little reward to show. Frank knew it was time for change.

This can be you as well. It is never too late to change your story.

How to build your Blueprint for Success

At the end of the day, when you cross the finish line (and we are talking retirement here!) you want to be satisfied in the knowledge you have achieved all your personal goals. This satisfaction all begins with the choices you make today. It all begins with building your Blueprint for Success, today and well into the future.

I believe it is the duty of every trade and construction business owner to create a business that serves them through the generation of profit and lifestyle – a business that can operate without the owner.

The reason most tradie businesses fail is due to lack of planning, lack of financial awareness and limited managerial experience. Business owners who are struggling to get ahead on a day-to-day basis are unable to answer the following questions:

- What price do I need to charge out to guarantee a financial return on investment in time and money?

- Which customers are costing me money?

- How can I grow my business without increasing my headaches?

- How can I work less and earn more – working smarter not harder?

- What systems do I need to implement to stop the business from controlling my life?

- What do I need to do to ensure the business provides personal, financial and lifestyle rewards for me and my family?

At Cube Performance, we have designed a four-step methodology – the Blueprint for Success business coaching program – that will allow business owners to confidently answer these questions. Since 2007, the Blueprint for Success methodology has been implemented into over 5,000 thousand tradie businesses through our business training and coaching programs.

BLUEPRINT FOR SUCCESS COACHING PROGRAM

The Blueprint for Success business coaching program follows a four-stage framework (Clarity, Control, Confidence, Connection) that is designed to support the business owner in creating a meaningful business and purposeful life, while being financially rewarded.

The following framework outlines the stages, modules, and outcomes.

Stage 1 – Clarity modules:

1   Get Your Mind Right for Business:

- Business Owner First
- Controlling Your Calendar to Prioritise Time

2   Planning for Profit:

- Design Personal and Business Goals
- Create Action Plan
- Create 12-month Financial Return on Investment Prediction ('The CUBE' – my Business Intelligence software platform)

3   Develop Your Brand Plan – Who You Are:

- Define the 'Way We Do It Here'
- Identify Your Profitable Niche and Understand Their Problem
- Define Your Customer Promise – Your Guarantee

Know where you are going, know what to charge and when to say no.
Believe in the value of your time.
Prioritise.

Stage 2 – Control modules:

1 Set Up Your Performance Scoreboard – Real-Time Business Intelligence:

- Measure Performance Against Goals to Keep on Track (sync accounting and job management data)
- Predict Your Performance – Analyse Actual Performance with Historical Trends

2 100% Financial Transparency – Where Has All My Profit Gone

3 Implement Profit Performance Driver Processes:

- Individual Productivity
- Sales Pipeline Planning
- Cash Flow Forecasting

4 Educate Your Customer:

- Communicate Why You Are The Experts at Solving Their Problem
- Assist Your Customer in Making an Educated Buying Decision

5 Automating Your Processes:

- Map All Process – Define All Required Tasks and Role Accountability
- Automating Process with Software

In control at all times.
Processes deliver consistent performance and results.
Peace of mind.

Stage 3 – Confidence modules:

1 Power Up to Attract Great Team Members:

- Recruitment & Induction Process
- Set the Expectation – The 'Way We Do It Here'
- Empowering Your Team to Deliver Without You

2 Power Up Your Team:

- Set Up for Success – Performance Conversations

3 Power Up to Attract Great Clients:

- How to Accelerate Sales
- How to Increase Conversion Rates
- Planning & Preparing for Meetings

4 Protecting Your Farm:

- Legal Protection – Define Terms of Trade

5 Guarantee Your Results:

- Real-time analysis of cash flow, profit and sales performance ('The CUBE' – my Business Intelligence software platform)

Educated decision-making.
Leadership from within.
Building brand advocates.
100% belief.

Stage 4 – Connection modules:

1   Partnerships that Leverage Your Expertise:

- Identify Potential Industry Partners
- Develop Win–Win Partnerships

2   Reinforce Your Brand:

- Industry Authority – Key Person of Influence
- Reinforce Credibility – Community Engagement, Social Media, Videos, Events, Trade Shows

Having fun.
It is NOT about you.
Generating profit and building personal wealth.
Great satisfaction.

For more information:

To 'Score Your Business', visit:

www.cubeperformance.com.au

To find out how we can assist you in building
your 'Blueprint for Success', visit:

www.cubeperformance.com.au

To access a free trial for 'The CUBE'
Business Intelligence software platform, visit:

www.thecube.network

To contact Matthew, email:

matt@cubeperformance.com.au

www.ingramcontent.com/pod-product-compliance
Lightning Source LLC
Chambersburg PA
CBHW071202210326
41597CB00016B/1645